Plumber, Lecturer, Pacifist, Spy (?)
How Uncle Cyril Saved the World

Cyril Pustan 1929-1977

© Laurence Saffer
2022

Grosvenor House
Publishing Limited

This book is published by
Grosvenor House Publishing Ltd
Link House
140 The Broadway, Tolworth, Surrey, KT6 7HT.
www.grosvenorhousepublishing.co.uk

A CIP record for this book
is available from the British Library

ISBN 978-1-80381-049-2

Dedication

This book is for Sally who has mentioned Uncle Cyril so often during our marriage that I feel I already know him even though he died 13 years before I joined the family.

It is also for Daniel and Rebecca who I have little doubt would have loved Uncle Cyril had they had the chance to meet him.

And it is for any other family member, political "relative", or friend here, in Germany, or elsewhere, who may be interested to understand a bit more about him, in the hope that his memory will not fade with time.

Table of Contents

1

Introduction - How Uncle Cyril Saved the World - A True underdog's story

Cyril Pustan was a plumber. But he was no ordinary plumber. He was also a University Lecturer, a poet, a writer, a musician, a photographer, an actor, a communist, an atheist, a pacifist, and a vegan. He was also possibly a spy.

He took part in the 1961 European leg of the Walk for Peace from San Francisco to Moscow, was in Berlin when the Berlin Wall started to be built in August 1961, met Yuri Gagarin's family, and had tea with Nina Khrushchev, wife of Nikita Khrushchev, on 6 October 1961.

For all his adult life he was active amongst the peace activists who stood up to the world's superpowers. He was one of those who became the conscience for the world and made the most powerful in the world stop and think.

It is not a photograph album, although some pictures have been included. It is not a collection of his works, although extracts of his writings are included. It is not a detailed family history, but some background has been included. It is not a historical analysis of world events, but some context is included. It is an inadequate biography by an amateur of a man I wished I had met. I hopefully do some justice to a peaceful, loving man, who lived by his principles, and through his actions, was the plumber who helped to save the world.

Where possible I have tried to mesh the different sources together to give a chronological account. I have retained the grammar,

Americanisms, and any minor typographical errors in the sections quoted. I hope I accurately translated the documents written in German with the assistance of Google Translate and Google Lens. I have block italicised Cyril's words and italicised the words of others for ease of identification. Any errors are mine.

2

Early life

In the beginning

It all began on 5 January 1929 when Cyril (his Hebrew name was Sheftel) was born to Hyman (Chaim) Louis Pustansky and Esther Deborah Pustansky (nee Himmelfarb) in Whitechapel, London. Well actually it began before that as we are all the product of nature and nurture.

Cyril's parents

Chaim (Chaim Yehuda Aryeh ben Reb Shmuel) (also known as Chaim Leib) was born on 10 December 1903 in Smila (spelt Smeela on his documents and Smyela elsewhere) in the Ukraine which was then part of the Russian Empire and is about 100 miles south of Kiev. He arrived in the United Kingdom in 1912 and died on 16 November 1984.

Esther Pustansky (Esther Devorah bat Reb Yehoshua Hershel) was born on 2 January 1905 the daughter of Harris Himmelfarb and Sarah Himmelfarb (nee Klumens) in London and died on 8 November 1990. When writing to his sister Ella, Cyril referred to Esther as *"the old girl."*

Esther and Chaim's wedding on 25 March 1928

Chaim was recorded as being a Hebrew Teacher on his marriage certificate, Commercial Traveller on Cyril's birth certificate, Draper Dealer on Cyril's brother Sidney's birth certificate, Teacher of Hebrew and Cantor on his 1947 Aliens Certificate of Registration, and a Minister of Religion on Cyril's marriage certificate.

Esther was recorded as being a dressmaker on her marriage certificate, and a factory worker prior to her marriage on Cyril's application for an extension to his East German Residence permit in 1964. She was much more than that as she became a wife, mother, and grandmother. She was also a homemaker, which with 8 children, was a full-time job in itself. She also loved watching snooker even though she only had a black and white television and could not differentiate between the different coloured balls without the commentary. She was a member of the Labour Party.

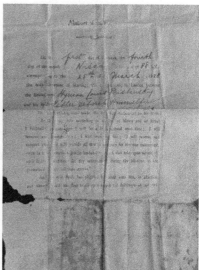

Chaim and Esther's Ketuba and English extract

Cyril's grandparents

Chaim's parents were Rabbi Samuel Pustansky and Etel Pustansky (nee Moshensky) who married in about 1901 and had 7 children.

Samuel was born in Kiev in 1882, brought Chaim to London to escape the pogroms, and died in 1948. Etel and the other 5 children joined them in 1923. Samuel was a noted Talmudist and scholar who wrote 4 religious commentaries - Sefer Rashbash, Beer Shmuel, Rashba, and Sefer Torah Shabtai. Etel was a nurse who died of typhus.

Esther's parents were Harris Himmelfarb who was born in Russia in 1867 and died in London in 1933, and Sarah Kluman (Klooman) who was born in Russia in 1875 and died in London in 1954. Harris was a collector for the Great Garden Street Synagogue.

Samuel   Etel

Cyril's great-grandparents

Samuel Pustansky's father Simon (Shabtai) was born in 1863. He married Esther-Rifka. She was born in 1862 and was the daughter of Simon's brother Chaim. Simon died in London in 1921 and Esther-Rifka in 1928. Cyril was named after Simon as Sheftel is the Yiddish version of Shabtai.

Simon had been wealthy, owned sewing workshops, and was very religious. Through his partner's mismanagement he became bankrupt.

Etel's parents were Solomon Moshensky and Rose Moshensky (nee Toplov).

Simon   Esther-Rifka

Harris Himmelfarb's father was Louis who was born in 1841 in Russia. Sarah's parents were Samuel Kluman who may have been born in 1837 and Jenni (Jane) Yudovin who may have been born in 1847. Jane was a draper and made underclothing.

Cyril's great-great grandfather

Simon and Chaim's father, and Esther-Rifka's grandfather, was Yehuda Poustjansky.

Back to Cyril

Cyril was born 9 ½ months after his parent's marriage and was followed by Sidney (26 June 1930), Stuart (September 1931), Ella (31 January 1935), Frederick (1938), Ivan (2 January 1942), Rosalie (22 September 1943), and Hilda (5 September 1946). The family lived in London, initially at 17 Plumbers Row, Stepney, then 20 Hemsworth Court, Hemsworth Street, Shoreditch, and finally 82 Hawksley Road in Shoreditch from 1971.

Early years

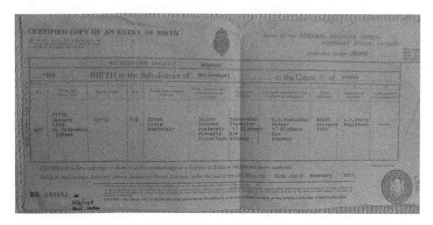

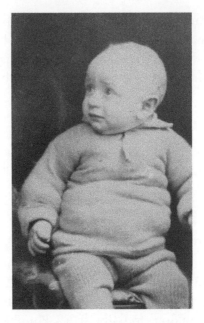

Cyril aged a few months

With his parents aged 1 and new-born brother Sidney

Cyril was educated at the Rochelle Street Elementary School in Bethnal Green. Schooling was compulsory from the age of 5 to 14.

Teaching was based on reading, writing and arithmetic. Chalk boards were the medium of teaching and sometimes writing for the children. School meals were not universal with children bringing in sandwiches, baked potatoes with their name carved on, or going home for lunch. Lines and being hit with a ruler were methods of enforcing discipline. Football with jackets for goals, skipping with a washing line, conkers, and hopscotch were games played in every street with children often outside with little if any adult supervision all day long. Comics and boardgames filled the time in poor weather. And in the tight knit communities each looked out for the other.

In 1937, Cyril came 11th out of 34 and was noted to be a *"very troublesome and untidy boy – good worker"*. In 1939 he came 20th out of 39 and was still *"very untidy in bookwork but otherwise making good progress"* and his conduct was *"excellent"*.

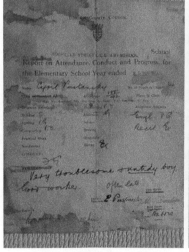 

1937   1939

Aged about 9 in 1938 with Sidney and Uncle Joe (Esther's brother)

In his autobiographical account of his experience of the war and leaving school he wrote that;

"until September 1939 life must have been fairly normal. Then came the war. The school I attended was evacuated away from London. I was billeted in a house with a local whore. Every night she dressed up and went to the pubs cadging drinks and soliciting clients from among servicemen stationed in the area...

I remember the first day we arrived in this town after a six or seven hour train ride, the first train ride I ever had. The local organising committee seemed at a loss as to what to do with us. They took us from door to door trying to find people to accommodate us, and this woman took us in. We had been given food parcels which she took and we never saw again. Four, two of my brothers" Sidney and Stuart *"my eldest sister"* Ella *"and myself slept in one bed. Sometimes when she came back from her nightly outings she was not too intoxicated, she would look into the bedroom, her eyes were glassy, and her breath filled the room with the sickening smell of alcohol. The first night my four year old sister wet the bed she got a good hiding.*

Our hostess said the money provided for our maintenance was inadequate and fed us accordingly. She said, "I get a penny farthing per person per meal and I'm losing money on every meal I give you."

Our schooling was reduced by half. The London children went to school half a day and the local children the other half of the day.

Several weeks later my mother came down to visit us, saw the situation and took us back home. It seemed like we ate for a whole week without stopping."

Cyril does not mention the far happier time when he stayed with his cousin Etel and her family in Luton with Sidney, Stuart, and Ella.

He then discusses his life in London after the evacuation fiasco.

"From October nineteen thirty nine until June nineteen forty two I attended no school. There was or seemed to be little control by the educational authorities and this coupled with the fact of my father being ill for a long period of time gave me a sense of freedom. I was able to wander through the streets of London for hours on end. Past the heaps of rubble, the scattered debris, the smouldering ruins of buildings and houses, and watch the rescue workers searching for the victims of the nazi bombardment. To earn pocket money I scrubbed floors. Interesting hours were spent distributing leaflets calling for a second front to help our gallant Soviet allies struggling single handed against the fascist armies

and attending the gigantic rallies where outstanding leaders... as well as refugees from Germany and other occupied countries spoke."

"I had come back to school six months earlier" than the local education authority committee meeting in June 1942 which had been arranged to discuss his future prospects *"because it was necessary to officially leave school before I could start full time employment. The six months were all wasted months, the one burning ambition I had was to join the army or the navy and take an active part in the war but I was too young."*

In a different version of his account he added;

"It was getting near the end of 1942 and near the end of my school days. Actually my school days had been brief. Today I regret how brief they really were."

He was at the Colombia Road Senior School in London's East End until December 1942 when he left just before he turned 14. He had only had 6 months of school education from when he was 10 ¾ years old.

In a lecture he gave in about 1965 he said;

"One of the few things I can recall about my schooling viewing it in retrospect is that it was a very poor schooling indeed. The arithmetic lessons were do as you please. No attempts were made to teach any mathematics – you were given an arithmetic book to work from and when you wanted to check your answers the teacher had a key from which you checked your answer yourself. English instruction – non-existent. Nobody who left this school knew what a noun was or a verb. History, hopeless although one teacher did attempt to tell us something about the feudal system on one occasion. ...Maybe the war years could be blamed for this state of affairs, maybe with the uncertainty of times the teachers could not be bothered to exert themselves, but the deplorable

conditions of illiteracy among the post war adolescents demonstrated that the type of education I received was more widespread that had hitherto been accepted by the knowalls."

His experience of the Blitz

In his essay "London's Burning" written in 1977, he writes of his experience in the Blitz through the eyes of John, an 11-year-old boy. At the time of the Blitz, Cyril was 11.

"Ting-a-ling-a-ling, ting-a-ling-a-ling, ting-a-ling-a-ling. A fire engine clanged along the main road, which was at the end of the street. John, aged 11, heard it clearly as he stood in the doorway of his parents house. The rest of the family were in the Anderson shelter out in the backyard. Across the street the houses were outlined against the red and orange sky. To John, the houses were no-man's land. Beyond them London blazed. Somewhere behind there held in a red crackling fist was the rest of Shoreditch, the city of London, the West End and whatever else there was that lay beyond. John had neither fear nor the sense to be afraid. He was convinced that as long as the houses opposite remain standing, all was well, at least, this side of no-man's land.

Glowing embers of wood drifted in the breeze. John watched them float at roof height. Occasionally one of them would splutter and fizzle out leaving a trail of smoke which lingered awhile…

Ting-a-ling-a-ling, ting-a-ling-a-ling, another fire engine, a fireman swinging the bell-rope, and on its way to somewhere.

The lull was over. Gunfire rumbled in the distance. The guns were watchdogs that growled at intruders, and the intruders were returning. The chant of their unsynchronised engines filled the night with their vibrant message: "We're coming! We're coming…!

The gunfire grew louder, louder, more vibrant, more determined. The distant gunfire could have been mistaken for a far-off thunderstorm, but the salvos which spewed skywards from nearby A.A. guns, sound like snarling thunderbolts.

A searchlight prodded the low-lying horizon trying to pierce the redness, but it poked in vain. Other searchlights played their beams criss-cross-wise into the night. A plane dived towards the blazing inferno of London. Searchlights caught it and held onto it. White puffs appeared around it. The plane pulled out of the dive, dropped a load of incendiary bombs and climbed back into the sky pursued by the sweeping searchlights.

People came out of the houses and ran towards a nearby street shelter...

The noise of the approaching bombers grew louder. The 'plops' of falling incendiary bombs were like heavy stones splashing onto water...

The street shelters planted with apparent haphazardness on suffering London, were for a while scoffed at. In time the Londoner became used to seeing them everywhere he went. Bumping into them in the blackout was accepted as part of the war effort, as was food rationing, the call-up, or air raids...

From nowhere a light dramatically appeared. It hung in the air. It was golden yellow. It was brighter than the fires. Brighter than the searchlights; brighter than the moon and all the stars. How was it able to stay where it was? Was it attached to one of the planes? Were the pilots able to see all that lay below them? Did this light move in straight lines? Could it pass through the walls of the shelter? Could it pass through the houses and beyond the houses? And where did the straight lines lead to? And if there were no straight lines, where did unstraight lines lead to?...

An express train hurtled through the air, its shrill whistle blasting at full power and every piece of metal in it rattling frantically. There was a flash and a violent explosion, and another, and then another.

The houses across the street in the street itself lifted and came towards John. John crouched ... Everything stood at a stupid angle. John waited for the world to topple. For the safety belt, that strip of no-man's land to collapse. But it balanced skewwise on tiptoes, balanced and continued to balance... An invisible hand pushed against oncoming calamity, and calamity reluctantly yielded and reeled back onto its heels again.

The houses had been hurt and shed loud tears: tinkle, tinkle, tinkle, and the pavement was littered with glass. And the houses heaved and coughed and the street was filled with dust...

More glass was falling. The dust was getting thicker. The flare was lost in gloom. Aircraft continued circling overhead. The guns were still firing..."

Career guidance

In his autobiographical account of his experience of the war and leaving school he wrote that;

"I decided to ask my mother what she thought I should become, she thought perhaps a job in a factory, maybe a clothing factory as a machinist where it was warm in the winter and dry. My father who had the problem every year of looking for a plumber to repair the burst pipes in the house thought it would be a good idea if I became a plumber, and my father was boss in the house. The labour exchange sent me out to several places but all were looking for a boy to sweep the floors and make the tea, these were just dead end jobs, there were no prospects of learning a trade and after a year or two you would be dismissed to make room for another boy. The Labour exchange could find nothing suitable.

So my father took matters into his own hands. He went to several different builders merchants to ask if they knew anyone who wanted a plumber's mate. He stopped workmen pushing builders trucks and eventually found me a job.

On Friday December the eighteenth I attended school for the last time. It was a particularly memorable occasion because the headmaster had brought for this day some gramophone records to play to the school, among them were records by Paul Robeson, Gigli, Mozart, Handel, Elgar, Menuhin. It was my first introduction to good music."

Growing up in war time Britain was the only childhood Cyril had. A childhood of the ultimate clash of ideologies, rations, bombs, disrupted education, and women keeping the economy going and running most homes. His home was of course different. Chaim's immigrant and refugee past fleeing pogroms, not serving due to his age, and his religious life, inevitably impacted on Cyril's thinking. Money was tight.

The Communist Party had increased in membership from about 16,000 in 1939 to about 56,000 by 1945. Two MPs were elected in 1945 and its 21 candidates received an average of 14.6% of their constituency vote. In the Local Council elections in 1946 it received over 500,000 votes and increased its number of Councillors from 81 to 215. It was a party on the rise. It was attractive to many such as Cyril.

3

Working life

In his autobiographical essay on his early years he continues,

"On Monday the twenty first of December three weeks before my fourteenth birthday I began work and became a mate to Bob the plumber. He was a skilled man, well read, self-educated, a staunch trade unionist and a communist. The day I began work, I too began my education so long neglected."

His various CVs identify that Cyril was a plumber's mate from 1943 to 1948, a journeyman plumber until 1955 at W Barford and Son in London, and then a self-employed master plumber until 1959. He initially earned £6 a month as an apprentice when he was 14, £40 a month as a plumber, and by the time he was a master plumber he was earning £80 to £100 a month. His CV identified that he also worked as a substitute teacher from 1950 to 1952 although I can find no record to confirm this, and it can only relate to substituting at Hackney Technical College on plumbing courses.

Between 1945 and 1955 he also attended Hackney Technical College in London and took numerous plumbing related courses leading to a multitude of City and Guilds Certificates.

In a lecture he gave in about 1965 he said about his application to join a trade union;

"When I and a friend applied ... for membership we were both 18 years of age and contrary to all that was right and holy we were working as tradesmen in a room of about 150 men, many of them

hostile. They began to ask us questions about how much are you earning and so on and so forth. Then we had to wait outside the room while they discussed our case. Eventually the secretary came out to tell us that we could not be accepted because the rate of pay was 2/11 ½ per hour" 2 shillings and 11 ½ pence – the equivalent of 15p *"and we were earning 2/11 per hour. Incidentally it was only that week the rate had been increased the odd half penny. However the deficiency in pay was adjusted and at the next lodge meeting we became members."*

At the workshop

Working outdoors

The thinker, poet, and political activist

Cyril was not just a plumber. He was a thinker and poet, and by the age of 16 already had political views that would steer him for the rest of his life, and a desire to learn and write. Ella said he was influenced by a teacher at school to be a communist. In October 1945 he wrote a poem seeking unity among workers following the defeat of fascism.

"From the free peoples of the West, to the free peoples of the East,
and to all those of you who helped destroy the fascist beast
The sanguinary battles you so valiantly fought and won,
With the significance of our unity must not fade like the sinking sun.

Those who under the jackboot of the dictators have had to live
and those who in the course of freedom have willingly give
all that was theirs to the course of a people's great victory
In order that we who survived might still yet be free.

The fascist hordes in the field have been decisively defeated
But not all their obsequious lackeys have yet been unseated
It is now time that this was done, twould be a great gain
It would show that the workers sacrifices had not been partially
in vain.

Those who think that the unity we ultimately brought about
Amongst the three great allies can now be done without
Would do well to note that had we had it before
There would not have been any carnage, nor any world war.

All who endeavour our essential unity to bring to nought
Are the very same elements to whom injustice they sought,
a means of reaction, a force on whom they could depend,
to which coercion, style, the workers leftward trend.

But now things are most definitely not the same
Although the old clique are still trying to play their game,
and the very just move on the board that they can see
is that in order to succeed, they must split the big three.

The toiling masses of the world are most completely aware
and any who dare seek to part them had better take care,
For they know that only our great unity decided the war,
and it will only be unity that will prevent it anymore."

S. Schichliche wrote on 14 June 1973 that *"since 1943 Mr Cyril Pustan got an insight into Marxist theory by attending lectures and courses at the Marx Memorial Library in London."*

Cyril was a member of the Communist Youth Association of England from 1943 to 1947, a Board member of the Shoreditch Communist Party Youth Committee from 1944 to 1947, the Communist Party in 1947, a branch officer of the Plumbers Trade Union in London in 1947, and the Society of English and German Democratic Republic (East German) Union from 1948 to 1962. Ella said he was once refused a job because he was a Communist.

The minutes of the Communist Party in 1946 note the internal discussions regarding whether to affiliate to the Labour Party, a discussion Cyril will have been involved with at local and Youth Association level. A key element of Communist Party discussions in that period revolved around the view that *"it is the Soviet Union and the camp of Peace which strive unceasingly for Peace and the Anglo-American imperialist bloc which strived to unleash a third world war"* as summarised by John Mahon, the London District Secretary, in his Political Report of 7 September 1952, the peace theme being one that ran throughout Cyril's life.

Cyril wrote about Karl Marx saying;

"In September 1867 the first volume of Capital was published. It was an edition of only 1,000 copies and printed in German. Today the book is known throughout the world and has been printed in many languages, and anybody who is anybody even if he has not read Capital knows the name of the author. How many people know the amount of work that went into the compiling of one of the greatest books of all time? Or how many people know of the sufferings undergone by Marx during his many years of poverty...Because of his poverty his three youngest children died. His wife who came from a wealthy family related to the British nobility had been his childhood sweetheart. She had married him despite the objections and hostility of her family."

21

National Service

In his application to renew his residence card in East Germany in 1964 he wrote that in 1947;

"I received the draft for the military and because of my opposition to the British government's foreign and colonial policy, I did not register for compulsory military service. It was only a matter of time before the state authorities would arrest me, and under the circumstances I thought it would be better to revoke my membership" of the Communist Party. *"Nevertheless I continued to contribute to the party funds, sell literature and promote the parties candidates in elections, take part in demonstrations etc."*

Cyril was eligible for National Service. He would have received his call up papers around 5 January 1947. He would have been required to register sometime after that. Instead, he attended Hackney Technical College continuously from 1947 to 1955. This was permitted deferment. He was not unpatriotic, and his view was reflected in the Report to the Communist Party Youth Conference on 28 May 1953 that *"Young people are patriotic, they love their country, they want to see it independent, out of this dirty American grip."*

In 1949 he was awarded a Diploma in Elocution from the London College of Music which helped him enormously in some of his later activities.

He changed his name by deed poll from Pustansky to Pustan on 20 May 1955. He paid £2, 4 shillings, and 6 pence, which is the equivalent of about £61 today.

He was now 27 and outside the regular call up range. His various CVs and accounts suggest that he continued working as a plumber and simply avoided it. National Service ended in 1960.

Regina Fischer wrote to Ella on 1 January 1980 regarding the army that "*Cyril would not go in after the war, what for?*"

Political backdrop

Life in post war Britain was difficult. Over 250,000 service personnel and 60,000 civilians had died. Many others were physically and emotionally damaged. A quarter of the national wealth had been spent on the war. Over 500,000 housing units had been destroyed by bombs. Five million service personnel were demobilised. Stresses on family life abounded with many women seeking to continue to enjoy working life while men sought to return to work. The post war divorce rate boomed with 60,000 applications alone in 1947. Rationing on some goods continued until 1954.

The Labour Party landslide in 1945 led to the creation of the NHS and Welfare State. Nationalisation led to 20% of the economy being taken over by the state. The Education Reform Act of 1944 which raised the school leaving age to 15 came too late for Cyril.

Rebuilding continued after Labour lost the 1951 election to the Conservatives following the collapse of the Liberal vote. The Communist Party, who Cyril supported, had slipped backwards in its support and garnered only 21,640 votes in total, and in 1955 only 33,144 votes. The economic boom enabled Cyril to use his plumbing skills to aid in the house building and repair programme. Incomes and spending power increased, and the standard of living improved. In 1952, 4,000 Londoners died from lung and heart disease caused by a 5-day smog bank. Cyril lived in London through that.

Class division was evident in clothing, educational opportunities, employment routes, and property ownership. Cyril was very much Working Class.

The Cold War which began in 1947, formation of NATO in 1948, and former Colonies seeking independence from Western powers, were the backdrop to the new international order, with the Soviet Union being demonised in the West. That demonisation conflicted with Cyril's political beliefs and world view.

It was against that backdrop that Cyril's political activity was relentless. On 10 August 1965, Kay Beauchamp, who was a leading light in the Communist Party and helped found the Daily Worker which later became the Morning Star, wrote that "*Cyril Pustan has been known to me for a number of years (since 1943). He has long been a staunch supporter of the Communist Party and has helped us in a number of election campaigns.*"

Festivals

Cyril may well have attended the 1951 Festival of Britain in London, but it was not the only Festival highlighting the nations organisers wish to showcase achievements.

In his application to renew his residence card in East Germany in 1964 he wrote;

"In 1955 and 1957 I became a delegate to Warsaw and Moscow from my union group and was sent to the youth festival."

The 1955 Youth Festival was held in August and lasted 5 days, although with events wrapped around it the total festivities lasted 2 weeks. It was the first to be held in Poland. The previous ones were all held in Warsaw Block countries being Czechoslovakia, Hungary, East Germany, and Romania. It was designed to be a meeting place for Eastern European communists and comrades from Western Europe, Asia, Africa, and South America, but in the eyes of the West was a propaganda exercise. It was the 5th such festival. More than 30,000 people from 114 countries participated, of whom 785 were from the United Kingdom. The motto of the festival was *"For peace and friendship - Against the Aggressive Imperialist Pacts"*.

It was reported in the Daily Worker which carried regular articles throughout the event, that the British delegates stayed in 3 large schools that had been turned into hotels. There were dining rooms, tennis courts, a football pitch, a swimming pool, 40 indoor theatres, 25 open air theatres, and 29 cinemas.

Stan Levenson, the Secretary of the British Youth Festival Committee wrote in *"British Youth in Warsaw"*, that;

"There were organised activities for all tastes - Ballet, jazz, folk music, singing, dancing, plays, circuses, excursions, visits, meetings of all sorts. There were the sports events of the Second World Youth Friendly Games...Although there were many hundreds of organised activities, we could spend our time as we wished.

Many visited Polish families, or just went swimming, or went wandering around Warsaw, or went shopping, or just simply basked in the August sun. Some had the opportunity of visiting other Polish towns...Several hundred visited Oswiecim (Auschwitz)..."

There were meetings, social visits, and trade meetings by occupation with delegations from other countries.

Stan wrote, *"Our Festival was something special. Not only because it was exciting and stimulating, but because it told a special story. The story that young people from all lands of all ideas, can live together in peace."*

Frances Miller wrote about the meeting between the delegations from the United States, China, France, Russia and the United Kingdom on 10 August where the theme was *"What the youth and the youth organisations of our countries can do in the cause of peace, friendship, co-operation and the furthering of understanding between the people's of the 5 Great Powers."*

Leslie Kaye from the Executive Committee of Mapam wrote that there *"were over a thousand other young Jews from 44 different lands...the meeting arranged by the Jewish Cultural Committee of Poland was a most moving experience..."*

1956 was a year with a heady mixture of world turmoil. Morocco and Tunisia gained independence from France. Fidel Castro declared war on the President of Cuba. Britain and France instigated the disastrous Suez Crisis. The Soviet Union crushed the Hungarian Revolution.

The 1957 Youth Festival was held from 28 July to 11 August. It was the 6th such festival. It attracted 34,000 people from 131 countries. Its motto was *"Peace and Friendship"*. It was a festival of athletics, music, and culture with an exhibition of fine arts where 3,000 works from 50 countries were exhibited.

There were exhibitions including of plastic arts, art, photography, and philately. There were 350 to 400 planned activities per day. It was reported in the "*Daily Telegraph*" on 16 August that "*Each member of the British party paid £47 to cover travelling, board and lodging.*" The opening programme in Lenin Stadium lasted more than 6 hours and started 1 hour late. Among those present were Secretary General Khrushchev of the USSR, and his successor Leonid Brezhnev. Reports were unanimous that Muscovites were overwhelmingly kind and hospitable to the delegates.

There were suggestions that the Festival should be boycotted including by Cristopher Mayhew MP writing in The Times on 24 October 1956, and supported by among others, the National Union of Students, and the Youth Department of the British Council of Churches.

The Daily Worker noted that there were 1,650 or 1,700 participants from all over the United Kingdom. This included delegations of miners, teachers, engineers, students, railway workers, and many Christian denominations including Quakers. They were able to talk freely to Soviet citizens. There was ballet dancing and a performance of Swan Lake, pipe bands, visits to Churches and factories, and a tree planting ceremony in Freedom Park. Some met Mr Khrushchev. There was a grand ball where Auld Lang Syne was sung. Participation in the Festival was not supported by the Labour Party, it being a Communist sponsored gathering, as confirmed by the Secretary Morgan Phillips in a letter of 9 April 1957.

Gleb Tsipursky noted in "*Socialist Fun – Youth, Consumption, and State-Sponsored Popular Culture in the Soviet Union 1945-1970*" that "*To weaken the festival's legitimacy, US and UK officials strongly discouraged their citizens from attending, though they did not ban travel to it, lest such repressive measures undermine the idea that they defended the values of liberty and democracy.*"

It was reported in "*Derniere Heure*" an Algerian journal on 6 August 1957 that "*On the Saturday, in the Big Synagogue in*

Moscow, more than half of the Israel delegation attended the religious service. Several thousand of Soviet Jews joined them or gathered on the route leading to the Synagogue."

Paul Jansen wrote in *"Pas a pas" (77/78) "Les Maisons des jeunes et de la culture" at the Moscow Festival"* that *"The official programme was very varied: meetings between countries, professional or interest meetings, national galas, shows of all kinds, competitions, sports, games... We were embarrassed by the range of choice. And we had already asked to do even more things: to visit a special building to meet a theatre or cinema figure, etc."*

In the *"Declaration of the International Committee of the VIth World Festival of Youth and Students for Peace and Friendship"* it was said that *"In Moscow and at other places we visited numerous factories, co-operative farms, working places, schools, and social institutions. Soviet boys, girls and their elders received us with a hospitality that touched everybody's heart deeply. They made us acquainted with their life and work."*

It was opined in *"Die Welt"* on 13 August that *"Anyone who came as a Communist will also leave as a Communist, not least because the improved living conditions of the Soviet population and the loosening of total dictatorship are everywhere visible, and not merely as part of a licensed folly for the Festival..."*

It was opined in the *"News Chronicle"* on 7 August, that *"The high jinks in Moscow make agreeable reading. Hatred seems to have taken a back seat and the young people drawn from nearly all the nations of the earth appear to be finding a unity which their elders seek in vain. But, sadly, it must be said that this is only a superficial view. The underlying tension and hostility between the West and Communist worlds persist...to the Kremlin the Youth Festival is a weapon in the cold war."*

At the meeting of Soviet Jewish Writers, Yosef Rabin from the USSR expressed optimism about the revival of Yiddish culture in the USSR.

Ella said that when he came back from the Festival, Esther asked him where his clothes were. He said he had left everything behind as the people there had nothing. He really did give people the shirt off his back.

Other activities

In 1958 Cyril trained at the Lucas-Tooth Gymnasium, whose main aim was to *"train young men to become qualified Instructors in Physical Training and to act in that capacity in Boys' Clubs, Brigades, and other youth organisations etc."*

Cyril at the gym far left bottom row

From 1959 to 1961 he worked as an overseas telegraphist at the Post Office on London.

His work did not interfere with his political activism.

He was a member of the Campaign for Nuclear Disarmament (CND) and one of thousands who took part in the CND marches from Aldermaston in Berkshire to Trafalgar Square in London at Easter 1959 where the rally was attended by 60,000 people. He was on the same 4-day march, sometimes through heavy rain, in 1960 where the rally was attended by 70,000 people.

He participated in the march to and sit-down demonstration at RAF Wethersfield in Braintree Essex in 1961 which the British Government provided to the US Air Force as part of their NATO commitment, and where over 800 demonstrators were arrested and fined by specially set up Tribunals. The demonstration was filmed on British Pathe and British Movietone News, although Cyril cannot be seen on either. One of the organisers of the demonstration, Pat Pottle, was later prosecuted for assisting George Blake escape from jail. Blake was a spy in MI6 but worked as a double agent for Russia.

This was not the only sit-down demonstration Cyril took part in as he did so at the Defence Ministry at Whitehall.

The family man

His sister Ella and Max's wedding on 20 April 1958

Cyril with Chaim and Esther toasting Max and Ella

Uncle Joe (Esther's brother), Cyril, Chaim, Sidney, Stuart, Ivan, Hilda, Esther, Auntie Rae (Joe's wife), Rosalie at Ella's wedding

4

The Walk for Peace to
Moscow of 1961

So how did Cyril, a London plumber, end up on the Walk for Peace to Moscow, and have tea with Mrs Khrushchev.

The international events that wrapped around the Walk

1960, 1961, and 1962 were significant years of world turmoil and tension between the USA and USSR, a brief timeline of which is required to understand the importance of the Walk and why Cyril and the other walkers felt that he had to act as he did. In some accounts it is called a March.

In the months leading up to Cyril joining the Walk, on 3 January 1961 President Eisenhower announced the suspension of Diplomatic and Consular relations with Cuba. There was an explosion at an atomic reactor testing station in Idaho killing 3 workers. On 9 January Britain announced they had uncovered the Soviet "Portland Spy Ring". On 20 January President Kennedy was sworn in.

On 1 February the USA tested its first inter-continental ballistic missile.

On 12 April Yuri Gagarin became the first man in space. On 17 April the USA invaded Cuba at the Bay of Pigs. It had failed by 19 April.

On 8 May George Blake was sentenced to 42 years in prison for spying for the USSR. On 25 May President Kennedy announced the Apollo programme to put a man on the moon.

On 4 June, the day Cyril took part in a Peace Rally at Trafalgar Square, President Kennedy and Secretary General Khrushchev began 2 days of meetings in Vienna and discussed nuclear tests, disarmament, and Germany.

The Walk for Peace begins in San Francisco

Cyril and Regina Fischer, one of those who walked the entire way, wrote an account on 20 October 1961, their wedding day, entitled *"The San Francisco to Moscow Walk for Peace gets there"*. They also gave the Hebrew year of 5543. The full account is annexed at the end of this biography as a historical record.

The Committee for Non-Violent Action (CNVA) organised the Walk. It was an American anti-war group, formed in 1957 to resist the US government's program of nuclear weapons testing. It was one of the first organizations to employ non-violent direct action to protest against the nuclear arms race. Its pioneering use of nonviolent direct action would have a significant influence on movements to follow.

A.J. Muste, the Chairman of the CNVA noted the difference in terminology as in Europe *"a walk means a stroll and a march means a walk."* Karl Meyer, one of the participants also noted the different terminology and said that *""March" is more commonly associated with more disciplined military, or large civil protest, formations, quite different from the more casual peaceful way we walked. The German, French, and some other translations of our leaflet used cognitives of "march", and the lead sign and other documents in the European phase called it the "American-European March""*. I use both expressions as Cyril uses both.

Bradford Lyttle explains that Regina came to be on the Walk through a friend enquiring on her behalf. She was selected as she was a registered nurse, could speak German, Russian and a little French, and was the mother of American chess prodigy and champion Bobby Fischer.

Cyril and Regina's account picks up the story;

"Late in November 1960, six men and two women drove from New York City to San Francisco...What had brought these people together, most of whom were strangers to each other, and why had they crossed the continent with such speed and determination? They had come to start a walk for peace that would last over ten months and take them over two continents and an ocean to Moscow, capital of the Soviet Union..."

The first section of all the accounts relate to the section from San Francisco to New York which began on 1 December 1960, which Cyril was not part of. They summarise the group in this way;

"Who were the people that finally marched into Red Square in Moscow on October 3, 1961? There were nine women and 22 men. The group ranged from a 19 year old youngster to a 48 year old grandmother" that being Regina. *"Americans made up half the group, the others coming from England, France, the German Federal Republic, Norway, Sweden, Belgium and Finland. Religious backgrounds included Unitarian, Roman Catholic, Jewish, Quaker, Lutheran, Christian Scientist, and Mennonite, as well as atheist and agnostic. Among the marchers were a professional model, a plumber,"* that being Cyril *"an anthropologist, an airplane design engineer, a secretary, a nurse, a teacher, an actor, a chemist, and a medical student. The group itself was independent of any political or religious affiliations.*

The peace walk was first conceived and organised by the Committee for Nonviolent Action (CNVA)..."

Bradford records that on the Walk across the United States, Regina was woken one night by a snake, on another occasion found a dead chicken and brought it to the group to eat, her smile was an asset when dealing with the authorities, and she was heckled while addressing a rally.

April Carter was the organiser of the European leg of the Walk from London to Moscow through the Committee for Non-Violent Action. Her papers reveal that the Walk was funded by various branches of the Society of Friends who raised their funds from their members, some Trade Union branches, and many small donations from individuals. There was extensive correspondence while the Walk was progressing through the USA with sympathisers in Europe in an effort to secure agreement from the various European countries they proposed to Walk through, and like-minded organisations who may be able to assist with logistical arrangements. They sought meetings with the leaders of all those countries, none of whom agreed to meet. They prepared leaflets and banners setting out their aims in 6 languages for use throughout the Walk.

The Walk policy was to;

1. Oppose equally the armaments of East and West
2. Support unilateral initiatives
3. Ask countries they pass through to abandon weapons of mass destruction
4. Oppose all war
5. Ask people to take personal responsibility through for example demonstrating, not paying taxes, or refusing to be conscripted
6. Protest through non-violent means if denied entry to a country,
7. Be prepared to be imprisoned
8. Not commit any violence on the March

Cyril enters the picture in London

Prospective walkers were sought from various European countries to join the 13 out of the 30 original walkers who were flying over from the USA. In the United Kingdom this was achieved through adverts in relevant papers.

April's papers show expressions of interest from throughout the United Kingdom. Participation was limited to enhance community cohesion, to improve the chance of admission into the countries they proposed to walk through, due to limited funding, and as the Soviet Union was not inclined to consider a group larger than 50.

Team members were *"chosen on the basis of their past experience of campaigning in their own country, their knowledge of languages, public speaking ability and other skills, their physical fitness, and in the light of the overall composition of the Team... All team members were required to bring with them: a warm sleeping bag; towel and soap; basic eating utensils (mug, plate, knife etc.); an extra pair of shoes and a pair of tennis shoes; many pairs of socks; some warm clothing to wear in Russia."*

And so Cyril applied.

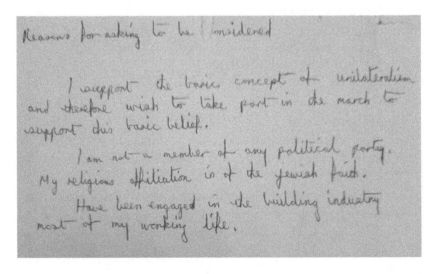

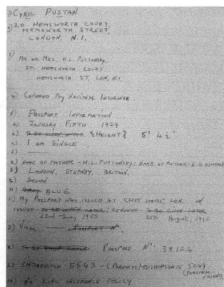

Cyril's application to join the Walk

On 24 May April wrote to him confirming that he was accepted as a member of the team for the whole Walk. He was required to attend a meeting on 27 May at 3pm at the Friends International Centre and be with the American walkers from when they arrived in London on 1 June 1961. They had many planning meetings and obtained supplies for the trip. It was there that he met Regina.

Regina and Cyril's account continues with the group's arrival in London;

"...the San Francisco to Moscow Walk for Peace has now become the American-European March strengthened by British and European team members. We hold many meetings to hammer out our future plans. We shop for equipment we will need in England and on the Continent. We have numerous public meetings, including a large one at the Friends Meeting House Euston Road. Finally, on June 4, we get an enthusiastic send-off from 6,000 at the rally in London's famous Trafalgar Square.

Standing high up on the plinth under Lord Nelson, we fight a losing battle with the pigeons calmly roosting above our heads. We look out into a sea of faces and banners. It is a thrilling moment. For the first time we can actually see in here that there are really people - many people- who take us seriously and back us up. Although we have just left America, we feel this is a true homecoming."

Trafalgar Square 4 June 1961
Cyril and Regina somewhere on the plinth at
the base of Nelson's Column

In his account, Jerry Lehmann noted the Trafalgar Square rally was attended by a crowd of 5,000 after which they marched to Hammersmith with a little over 3,000 supporters. The police estimate of the total number of marchers was 8,000.

In his application to renew his residence card in East Germany in 1964 Cyril wrote;

"In 1961 I was elected as the British representative by my collective of British peace groups to take part in the Peace March from San Francisco to Moscow."

Cyril and Regina's account of their now joint involvement continues;

"CND support brought out thousands to walk with the peace marchers to the outskirts of London. CND organisations continued to draw crowds, bring newspaper, radio and television publicity, and arrange public meetings, large and small all along the route of our 50-mile walk to Southampton. Many times hospitality and meetings were arranged with the Quakers. Along the route we had factory-gate and village-green meetings. A vigil was held at Aldermaston, the Atomic Weapons Research Establishment, which has become the goal each Easter of the British marchers for peace.

As we arrived in Southampton we got word ... that the Russians had agreed to let us in..."

Leading the walk in England – on the right

Jerry noted the lack of billboards, car junkyards, and heavy traffic. The police strolled along at the end of the group. The English were hospitable people with food and accommodation. Public meetings were seldom indoor or formal.

The Walk was covered by the British press including Peace News who carried extensive coverage throughout its progress.

Bradford noted that on 12 June they held an internal meeting to discuss application for membership in the team, and Cyril spoke at British Railways shops.

In the official biography of the Walk team members Cyril is described as;

"Cyril Pustan; 32; plumber, atheist; single;... First class City and Guilds Certificate in plumbing work, sanitary and domestic engineering. Member of Royal Society of Health and has a speech therapy teaching diploma. He is a local branch official of the Plumbing Trades Union and has been a delegate to several European countries. Has taken part in Aldermaston Marches and civil disobedience demonstrations in London."

In a separate short biography where eating requirements are identified, Cyril is one of those identified as a vegetarian and *"no eggs"*. He is recorded as being Jewish.

UK route

France

Cyril and Regina's account continued;

"The friends meeting house in Southampton was crowded when we said farewell before sailing on the British railways channel steamer <u>Normannia</u>. But when we arrived in La Havre on the morning of June 13, we were flatly refused permission to land. No reason was forthcoming, and finally, after notifying all the authorities, we held a protest demonstration in which four members of the team jumped overboard and swam ashore to distribute leaflets and speak briefly to the French people, while a fifth man jumped and remained on shore. The four who were rounded up by the police and returned to the ship persisting in their demonstration, jumped overboard again, and again were returned to the ship. On our second attempt a week later, on June 22, France again refused us entry and this time 19 of our group went over the side of the ship. All again were returned to England by the French authorities."

Cyril's account for the Tribune on 20 October 1961 adds more detail;

"Morning looms bright, the channel steamer is heaving and my blanket is soaked with spray. The voice of our fellow in charge tells us to be ready to leave the ship shortly.

Then the same voice several minutes later says we don't leave the ship shortly. Some fellows have come aboard, tall nice looking guys, bland smiles and sour faces. Say they represent a body called the French Government who have instructed them to instruct us that we can't land; and just to help us not to, they have taken our passports and given them to the purser to lock up. Why can't we land? Sorry, they don't know, just instructions, nothing to do with them.

A lookout is posted on the upper deck and the rest of the group are busy discussing what to do and how to do it. Who can we afford to leave in France for ten years and who do we keep with us?

The general idea is, we're going to swim - not the whole group, just four of us. I sit and calmly listen while the fight goes on for honours. Queen Fischer demands her rights and when Queenie gets to work, step aside boys, step aside. I don't have to. I can't swim...

Bob Kingsley jumped and was headed toward an iron ladder leading from water to land. Queenie held her nose and jumped. The plop she made scared Bob, who had been told earlier the police might shoot. He thought they were shooting at him.

The others, a man and a woman, headed in a different direction, evaded a police launch and landed at a point 200 yards away. Now Bob helped Queenie to land, distributed his leaflets from a plastic bag, saw the police take Queenie away and forget about him. He was whisked away by supporters and it was going to be several days before we saw him again.

Queenie was brought back to the ship and minutes later the other two arrived through the dock gates, the man being roughly dragged up the gangplank. They must have been trying to smooth out the rough edges on his back.

A decision was taken to jump later and the group went over at 7.30. This time they were not returned but taken to the police station and detained. At 11 p.m. they were brought back.

A young girl, an American student, who had come on board to visit us, left the boat to return to her hotel in La Havre but was savagely attacked by the police who threw her up the gangplank, one of them standing poised at the foot looking as if he would kill her. His face was snarled with venom and brutality.

Many of the passengers became wild at the police action. The first Le Havre demonstration was over. I went down to the restaurant for supper, hadn't eaten all day."

Jerry's account added context to the French reluctance to allow the Walk given the unpopularity of the Algerian war and French nuclear policy, and lack of recognition in some quarters of the De Gaulle regime. Political demonstrations and meetings were forbidden. There were bombings and highways were blockaded.

Cyril and Regina's account continued;

"Newspaper photographers and television cameras recorded our protest in the waters of Le Havre. We hoped that in this way many people all over the world would realise how important it was to us – and to them - to raise the demand for an end to the arms race before the people of every nation, without Government interference. A BBC television man later told us that the French Government's intransigence had resulted in more people throughout the world learning about the San Francisco to Moscow peace marchers than if we had been granted permission to enter.

It was only later that we learned that the French Government had notified British Railways in advance that we would not be admitted to France."

Regina climbing out of the harbour in
Le Havre having cannonballed in

It was reported in *France-Soir*, that at least 2,000 French people were at the pier, the vast majority of whom were sympathetic, cheered the swimmers, and condemned the government for its refusal to grant them entry to France.

Cyril wrote that on the second attempt to enter France on 22 June;

"At 4 PM, three no-swimmers (myself included), finding owing to the high tide that it was impossible to jump from the boat to the quay, decided to go down the gangplank.

Three police stood at the bottom of the gangplank eyeing us intently, and then for an instant their attention was diverted and Wyn Evans made a dash and reached the dock. Susan and myself followed; when held by the police we sat on the ground and were dragged to the police van. The van travelled up and down for about an hour, taking aboard the swimmers who had landed. At the police station, I was dragged from the van and thrown into a room on top of several other people. The police inside the van had been friendly, but our refusal to walk into the station had annoyed them.

Half an hour later, several more swimmers were brought in. In the station the police were somewhat offhand but when Lyn Marsh had explained our position and why we felt forced to demonstrate, many of them appeared to be sympathetic towards us... telling us that they had to carry out their orders.

At 11 PM, the police informed us that we were going back to the boat. We were heaped aboard the van together with some stretchers, and back to the docks. A person would be pulled from the van into a stretcher and carried by two policeman aboard ship. Karl Meyer had been taken from the van and was being carried away, when from the window of the van I could see that the boat appeared to be moving and that the gangplank was being unlashed. The boat moved, leaving the gangplank free. Dockworkers and police made desperate efforts to hold it, but the counter-leverage was too powerful and the gangplank plunged over the quayside into the water. A shout went up and pandemonium seemed to break loose, people rushing all over the place; someone was in the water. I thought that Karl had fallen in but a moment later he was thrown back into the van and punched in the face. A few minutes later the boat moved off, leaving Karl Mayer, Lyn Marsh and myself still inside the van."

In the account recited by April that she had obtained having spoken to Cyril, she said that, *"One unfortunate aspect – which shouldn't be published in releases – is that the Captain cast off without hauling in the gang plank, and a stevedore who was on or near the plank was thrown into the water and badly bruised, and had to be rescued."*

Cyril continued, *"The van travelled down the road to the quay ... we were locked up, three men in one cell and the women in another... we were given a blanket each and tried to settle down for the rest of the night... There seemed to be no air movement in the ten by twelve room of ours, with its grilled windows, wooden sleeping platform, concrete walls and the galley trap in the floor. It had the smell and atmosphere of a neglected backstreet public urinal... The women who were two cells away from us spent most of their time laughing or singing, their plaintive voices floating through the grill that led to the artificial light from the passageway."*

In the account given by April based on what she had been told by Cyril, she added *"On the morning of the 23rd the group asked to see the British Consul. As the police wouldn't take responsibility for feeding them Cyril had to get £2 changed into Francs – and one of the police bought food for them with this money."*

It was reported by the Committee for Non-Violent Action that;

"Several of the demonstrators were very roughly handled by the police, particularly at points where they were not in the presence of the public. Those who were held in the French jail were in crowded cells with open sanitary facilities; however, many of the police officers were quite friendly."

Cyril continued *"June 24... At 2300 hours we were transported once again to the dock. There we met M. Colleu of the French Committee who thanked us. He said they felt we should not demonstrate on that evening as we had already done sufficient for the honour of France. So we went abroad unshaven, unwashed and unhappy that the French episode of our journey had ended in this way."*

In the account given by April based on what she had been told by Cyril, she added in relation to their departure that *"they agreed*

*not to make any further attempts to leave the boat. They also
agreed after discussion not to fray the tempers of the police any
further or risk a further incident with the gangplank, and to walk
from the van to the boat."*

Karl Meyer was one of those detained with Cyril for the 2 nights
and 3 days they spent in the cell at Le Havre. Cyril appeared to
Karl to be either a member of the Communist Party (which he was
not but had been), or a strong Soviet sympathizer. Karl said that
Cyril appeared to be quite taciturn, somewhat sullen in affect,
and with a belligerent streak to his personality. Cyril certainly
was taciturn as many referred to him being quiet. He spoke when
it was appropriate. And when he spoke, he did so as he had
something to say. It certainly was not a bad trait. As to sullen,
Cyril was a serious man, on a serious endeavour, and the Walk
was hard. But it was not a view shared by all as Dave Rich was
one of those who walked from San Francisco and remembers
that Cyril was a dedicated and courageous man, and a happy
and upbeat member of the group. Cyril told Dave about his life
as a labour leader and that he had been working for peace for
some years. And Karl was right that Cyril certainly did have a
belligerent streak to his personality as evidenced by what he did
during his life.

April Carter's papers reveal that there were concerns that as Bob
Kingsley had defied the agreement of the group for only 4 people
to jump in at Le Havre, he could have been planted by the CIA or
communists. They also revealed that the cost of repatriation to the
United Kingdom of each walker including Cyril was £4 per walker
per deportation so £8 in total. Letters were sent by British
Railways who owned the Normannia to the home address of each
individual walker seeking reimbursement, which must have come
as something of a shock to Esther and Chaim. The repatriation
was paid for by the Committee for Non-Violent Action.

The Walk was extremely well organised due to the open and
extensive negotiations with local communities and supporters.

However, the delay in getting started in France led to the timetable slipping and much reorganising.

Belgium

The group instead went to Belgium whilst waiting for French walkers to join them. It was reported by the Committee for Non-Violent Action that *"They were cleared promptly by immigration officials. Members of the Belgian Committee welcomed the March and accompanied them to Nazareth, an international peace centre near Rummen. Receptions and lectures were arranged at Nazareth."*

Cyril and Regina wrote;

"we laid drainage pipes and cleared away underbrush at a farm near Rummen, Belgium, to help prepare it for service as an international peace centre.

In Belgium we had the help of the Catholic Church for the first time. We ate and slept at many Catholic schools, convents and monasteries... outdoor meetings were held in the market places with the aid of our truck and loud-speakers going before us announcing them. Our indoor meetings were generally arranged in local coffeehouses or cafes, in keeping with the local custom.

Many Quakers and members of the War Resisters' International walked with us in Belgium. Meetings of several hundred persons were held in Brussels and Antwerp. We demonstrated before NATO headquarters in Brussels, and before the National Fabrique des Armes."

Caserne Prince Baudouin, Brussels – 3rd from the
left Ifan Wyn Evans, Karl Meyer, Lyn Marsh, Millie Gilbertsen,
then 2 to her right John Kruse, then 4 to his right Dave Rich,
Nils Petter Gleditsch, and finally Cyril

Bradford noted that on 10 July Cyril spoke at a meeting attended by townspeople in Tirlemont. A.J. Muste, the Chairman of the Committee for Non-Violent Action and its main organiser, had joined and was present at the talk.

The Committee for Non-Violent Action reported that *"Official receptions were given by the mayors of six towns. Newspapers, radio, and TV gave the March very good coverage; a feature story was carried by the official Soviet newspaper."*

International tensions continued to rise during the Walk. On 4 July a Soviet nuclear submarine suffered a reactor leak in the North Atlantic. On 25 July President Kennedy stated *"we will not be driven out of Berlin"* and urged Americans to build nuclear fallout shelters.

The map used by Cyril on the Walk in its protective case

West Germany (German Federal Republic)

Cyril and Regina wrote;

"On July 16 we entered the Federal Republic of Germany at Aachen. Many peace groups helped us in Germany …We slept and ate in youth hostels, private homes, houses of the Friends of Nature, Quaker meeting houses, and at the International Friendship House in Buekenburg, near Hanover.

Police escorts accompanied the march practically all the time; sometimes the police cars carried our rucksacks for some when we became tired. We had quite a few disagreements with the police over the slogans we could carry, which they felt had to be approved in writing every time. We also had some differences with the police when they re-routed the walk so it would not pass by military barracks or other military installations lying directly on the route. We tried very hard to obtain official permission to hold military protest demonstrations in West Germany but could not succeed."

Bradford noted that on 30 July while some attended demonstrations, Cyril would continue the walk.

Bee Herrick wrote in her account that on 31 July *"All walkers must carry their own packs. The van is kaput...Lunch is early and delicious. A fresh green salad breaks the monotony of bread and cheese 3 times a day (which is what we usually get unless someone offers us a meal)...A crate of milk has been left for us by the side of the road – anonymously. This is our lucky day. The belly god takes over...The Minden police attempt to reroute us for at least the fourth time since we have been in West Germany because of traffic or passing a military installation. We are not allowed "within shouting distance" of bases...All the Walkers sit very orderly and wait...It is a tense situation sitting on the grass, waiting. Then the police announce that we are allowed to continue but we are not without their "protection"...It's been a long, lovely, sunshiny day and we feel content, grateful that we have beds to sleep in tonight. We stop for a while trying to solve the world's problems and retire for the night pleasantly exhausted."*

Cyril and Regina continued;

"...on August 3 we arranged four simultaneous demonstrations against the War Ministry in Bonn, the Bergenhohne NATO military base, the Dortmund Brackell rocket base, and the Hanover recruiting headquarters. The police did not permit the Dortmund and Bonn demonstrations to be carried out as planned. Some of the demonstrators were arrested briefly, tried, and sentenced to brief sentences or fines, none of which were carried out.

Many Germans, usually between 50 and 60 at a time, walked with us along our route, especially on weekends...

51

Some spoke of how their thinking had undergone a long and painful change after their wartime experiences and the catastrophes that had finally put an end to the war. I felt it was a tribute to the essential goodness of people that these men today were sincere partisans of peace and would no longer support the military policies of their country..."

While on a visit to the site of the Belsen concentration camp and looking at the memorial and gravestones they wrote;

"While we were looking at these graves we could hear sounds like thunder coming from the Bergenhohne shooting ranges all around the area. Giant-size tanks were seen travelling along the roads. Planes and helicopters were overhead constantly. Truckloads of soldiers were coming and going. The terrible message of Belsen was, it seemed, being lost in the confusion."

In Cyril's essay "London's Burning" written in 1977 where he tells of his experiences though the eyes of "John", he writes;

"Some years later John visited a former Nazi concentration camp. His arrival coincided with a red sunrise. The whole open area of the former camp was covered with white pebbles, glinting as the first rays of the sun hit the ground. The guide picked up a pebble handed to him and said: 'It's part of human bone. They were burning so many bodies towards the end that they had no time to bury the ashes from the crematoriums.

John was so horrified at the enormity of it. His thoughts sprang back to a night of aerial terror over London... He thought of the dying embers he had seen and said to himself "And this is one of the places where dead embers finally come to rest.""

Walking through the border town just before
crossing into East Germany

On the Walk with Regina

East Germany (German Democratic Republic – GDR/DDR)

Lawrence S. Wittner noted in *"Resisting the Bomb"* the reluctance of the East German government to admit the walkers, due to their perception that West German soldiers' commanders were war criminals, whereas military service in East Germany is the honourable duty of every citizen.

Victor Grossman was living in East Germany at the time and remembered waiting for the walkers at the border to welcome them. After a delay, the walkers were admitted. Victor joined the walkers for 2 days during which time Cyril drove the lorry which contained the walkers' equipment as the walkers shared the non-walking duties to give rest time. Cyril discussed with Victor the mixture of political views of the walkers.

Cyril and Regina continued their account;

"On August 2 we crossed the border from Helmstedt to Marienborn in the German Democratic Republic. We were given a very friendly reception from the German Peace Council and found many people waiting to greet us. During our brief visit to the GDR great trouble was taken to provide us with good food, convenient places to sleep and opportunities to talk to people accompanying us on the walk or at public meetings or along the road.

Practically all the people expressed their horror of war, a desperate desire for peace and a deep fear that they might be attacked. All made clear their desire for a peace treaty which would demilitarise the whole area of Germany on both sides and which would guarantee that no former Nazi leader would ever again hold positions of leadership in West Germany. Their fears and desires seemed to be reasonable and based on realities. At no time did anyone express desire for revenge or any wish to force their way of life on West Germany.

We carried our signs and distributed our leaflets everywhere just as we had done in the West. 15,000 leaflets were distributed in the week we spent in the GDR."

Victor remembers that the East German authorities would not allow the walkers to go near major cities or military bases. Some of the walkers, instead of walking as agreed, went on bikes well off the determined routes to distribute anti-military leaflets to people in uniform. They seemed to know very well where Soviet and GDR soldiers were stationed. Cyril told Victor this and stressed that such distribution to men in uniform at their camps, had not been engaged in on the earlier, western stages of the walks.

Cyril and Regina continue, *"Unfortunately for us we came to Berlin just at the moment of the Berlin crisis - August 14, 1961."*

This was the day after the Russians began to build the Berlin Wall by putting up barricades preventing East Germans fleeing to West Germany and prompting an international crisis. The status of Berlin which lay geographically in East Germany but was divided with the USSR, USA, France and the United Kingdom each controlling a quarter had been the subject of debate and tension since 1945, and came to a head in 1961. It is estimated that nearly 4,000,000 East Germans had "escaped" to West Germany during that period and it was felt essential by the USSR and the East German government that the flow of people, and in particular well-educated young people, must be stopped as it weakened the state economically and led to a brain drain. It was into this turmoil that Cyril walked.

Bradford recounts the conversation he had with Herr Zack, representative of the Ministry of the Interior, who outlined the crisis in Berlin, said they were on the brink of World War 3, and said they would not be allowed to enter Berlin.

Cyril and Regina wrote;

"We were told that we would not be permitted to enter Berlin but could go by bus toward the Polish border, there to resume our walk."

"Cyril Pustan" and two others Astrid Wollnick and Ifan Wynn Evans said that the *"ultimatum was reasonable and they would accept it; they left our meeting. In our project, individuals were always free to do what they felt was right, but when they violated a team decision, they did so by withdrawing from the team. Cyril...understood this rule of our discipline and did not try to speak for the team."*

In his application to renew his residence card in East Germany in 1964 he wrote;

"I was one of the three members of this group who were given asylum by the GDR peace committee when the other participants were expelled from the GDR."

Nils Petter Gleditsch, one of the marchers who joined in London with Cyril, remembers that most of the marchers were disappointed that Cyril, Astrid, and Ifan chose to accept the barring ultimatum on them entering East Berlin. He thinks that the strict pacifist majority of the walkers, including most of the Americans, felt that some of the European marchers including Cyril, Astrid, and Ifan were motivated more by political concerns than by pacifism. Nils also remembers *"something going on between Cyril and Regina"*. Karl thought Cyril was probably not a pacifist.

Cyril had to leave the team and there had to be a decision to readmit him then they reunited in Poland.

Jerry noted the provision of accommodation in barns and classrooms, the excess of butter leading to stomach upsets, and the Red Cross support for medical assistance during their time in East Germany.

Jerry wrote about the endless negotiations about the banners and slogans that could be used during the march in East Germany and the complex negotiations that led to a resolution. He noted that Regina undermined this initially by putting on a disputed sign and offering to wear it. There was also concern about the press reporting, it being said that Cyril had asked for political asylum. He had not.

Poland

Cyril and Regina wrote;

"...on August 22 the team was reunited in Poland. The three who had refused to return to West Germany awaited the others at the border point.

From the moment of our arrival in Poland we felt that it was here we were receiving the warmest welcome of our entire trip. From the time we crossed the Oder river to our approach to the eastern border the Polish Peace Committee gave us unfailing courtesy, genuine friendliness and strenuous efforts to help us meet as many people as possible. Polish hospitality was far beyond anything we could have expected. The food was wonderful - often too plentiful and too good for our own good. We slept in beds every night, a record never equalled in America or anywhere else in Western Europe. Villagers invited us into their houses and asked us to let them hear from us in future. People met us all along the route with great interest. Students and teachers alike invited us into their class-rooms to tell them about our efforts for peace.

A visit to Auschwitz made a profoundly saddening and terrifying impression. Auschwitz was far off our march route but at our special request the Polish Peace Council arranged for us to make a special trip there and back.

The Poles gave us complete freedom of speech on the streets and on the radio. We handed out leaflets and carried our signs everywhere without question or interference. No effort whatever was made to add their own signs or leaflets. Every effort was made to organise public meetings for us. At any time we were free to speak to people, visit them in their homes, go to movies, theatre, shopping or do any of the things anyone might do visiting abroad. No police accompanied the walk. We demonstrated freely before the Ministry of Defence in Warsaw."

Regina and Cyril somewhere on the Walk

USSR

In September 1961 the Soviet Union announced that it was to recommence nuclear testing. This led to international condemnation. Lawrence S. Wittner noted that this may have been why they were allowed to walk and protest through the Soviet Union, and meet Mrs Khrushchev, and could not have happened without Secretary General Khrushchev's approval.

Cyril and Regina wrote;

"On the morning of September 15, a Saturday, we crossed the border from Poland into Russia. There was a long delay while we had to wait on the bridge over the Bug River between the two

countries. The Soviets had resumed bomb-testing and our time in the USSR had been cut from six weeks to three weeks. We did not know how things would be in the USSR after the overflowing friendliness, freedom and hospitality of Poland.

All of a sudden the wind came up, it got cold, and it began to pour. We felt dismal enough. But the rain stopped, we were given a signal to come through the barrier, and before we knew it we were being met by photographers, people were handing us bouquets of gladioli, and we were being ushered into a building that looked more like a private house than a border customs point.

Nobody bothered to look in our baggage. The room was crowded with representatives of the press, radio and TV, as well as the Mayor of Brest himself, and many officials of Soviet peace organizations, Intourist, and others. Actually, the Soviet welcoming committee was ready and anxious to get us started with dinner and a visit to the Brest Fortress nearby. But the walkers would not budge until a long list of their questions was gone over. The meeting must have stretched out for three or four hours, wearing us all out. The Russians politely starved while we munched away on buns and sandwiches thoughtfully provided for us in advance by our Polish hosts.

Finally, satisfied with the results of our negotiations, we all got up to start the march in the USSR...

That evening, after a fabulous feast in the Bug Hotel, replete with caviar and wine, not to mention vodka, we went to our first public meeting in the Soviet Union. The Trade Union House was packed. About 500 sat in seats, with many more crowding the doors and the hall...

Since the distance from the border of Russia to Moscow was so great (658 miles, 1054 km.) and we had only three instead of six weeks to do it in, it became necessary to work out a shift system...

At first the Russians insisted we must stay together as a group, as we had actually agreed to do prior to our coming. To meet this requirement, and at the same time cover the mileage, meant that all the walkers had to get up at 4:45 in the morning, eat and get out on the road, there to remain until at least perhaps 10pm. in order to be able to say honestly that the entire distance had actually been walked by some part of the team. Soon the two buses accompanying us began to look like hospital ambulances. While part of the team walked, the others lay on seats and on the floor trying to catch up on a few hours sleep until their turn to relieve the others. Evening meetings and entertainments kept the walkers going until 2am or 3am and some hardly bothered to undress before they reeled into bed.

Soon the walkers began dropping like flies - picked up by the ambulances they were being taken to hospitals with exhaustion, indigestion and general disintegration. In alarm, the Russians called an emergency meeting with the group. They tried to dissuade the walkers, urging that they walk their usual approximately 40 km. (25 miles) each day as a single group and then take the bus the rest of the way to their destination for the night. In vain they pointed out that much of the route to Moscow lay through sparsely inhabited swampland and forest. The walkers remained determined - a walk was a walk and it must be walked. The Russians shook their heads over this, to them, quixotic attitude and gave in. Thereafter they cooperated in every possible way with a three shift system asked for by the team starting at 3 a.m. and finishing about 8 p.m. enabling the team to complete the walk to Moscow on foot.

In the three weeks we spent in the USSR, a conservative estimate of the number of street meetings would be between one and two hundred. The average would be at least 100 people, often several hundreds to 1,000 or more...

On some days in populated areas in the Soviet Union as many as eight or 10 meetings would be held one after the other along the highway among the crowds gathering around the walkers. Sometimes three or four meetings would be going on at once, the number being limited only by the number of translators available or the ability of the walker to make himself understood alone. Sometimes walkers just started speaking to a few people and in two seconds flat huge crowds were around...

At Orsha the crowd had to be held back by a cordon, and at Gzhatsk I was cut off from the group by the crowd and had to appeal to a passerby to get me to the evening meeting where I was scheduled to be one of the group's speakers.

Speeches usually started around 8 or 9 pm and ended around 11 or 12pm, depending on whether our walkers came on time or were late. After the speeches came the entertainment, which could last until 1 or 2 in the morning...

In Russia, as in Poland, sleeping was always in beds. I do not recall having slept on the floor once in either country and had no more use for my sleeping bag...Most of the time in Russia we slept in hotels or schools, with fresh linen, blankets, and often, facilities for washing and laundry. At first we protested that beds were not necessary; we were used to roughing it and perfectly comfortable sleeping on floors. But our protests gradually grew feebler as we gratefully crawled into nice warm beds each night.

Medical care was always available and doctors appeared at the slightest whisper of a headache or upset stomach...I myself also landed in a hospital in Minsk, the Rosa Luxembourg Fourth Clinical Hospital. I was taken there when I was suddenly seized with cramps and vomiting, and in a few days of treatment and rest recovered completely. While there I was much impressed by the friendly, informal relationship between the doctors, who are mainly women, the nurses and patients."

Meeting the Gagarin family

Yuri Gagarin was the world's first astronaut, and in 1961 one of the most famous men on earth. Cyril and Regina wrote;

"On September 30 we met the Gagarin family in the evening meeting at Gzhatsk. They sat on the stage with the chairman of the meeting. Gagarin's sister, a nurse in a children's institution, spoke at the meeting. She was quite indignant over the stress abroad on cosmic travel for military purposes and stressed that her brother's achievements in the conquest of space were great contributions to world science."

With Regina and Mr and Mrs Gagarin

Moscow

Cyril and Regina wrote;

"Our arrival in Moscow was a joyous occasion, the weather warm, sunny, just right. The streets were crowded with people,

clapping, waving, some shaking our hands and thanking us, calling out to us, some in tears. Leaflets went like hotcakes.

We were surprised to see the broad, clean avenues, numerous speeding buses, the huge size of the housing developments everywhere, the crowded stores, and the floods of billboards advertising all kinds of plays, concerts, lectures, recitations, amateur talent programmes, and so on.

Our actual walk into Red Square and two hour demonstration there with our signs and leaflets were the high spot of our arrival. Dozens of foreign and Soviet correspondents, plus radio and television, recorded the scene as crowds milled about, asked us questions, pressed all kinds of badges on us and asked for ours in return. I could hardly believe that we had actually made it - that after all those months of walking we had really reached our goal. It was a wonderful feeling. The job was done, and well done...the Kremlin Clock chimed four and the San Francisco to Moscow Walk for Peace was officially over."

Cyril walking into Moscow
Third row on the left

Kutusovsky Prospect Moscow
Second row in the middle

Regina, Cyril, Bradford Lyttle, Mardy and Barton Stone

Red Square – Cyril's head can be seen in the middle second row
in front of a very tall Patrick Proctor and behind Scott Herrick –
Regina is looking up and Dave Rich is holding the banner

It was the end of the Walk, but meetings were arranged in Moscow with USSR's leaders such as Michail Gyeorgadze, Secretary of the Praesidium - the legislative authority when the Parliament was not sitting.

Tea with Mrs Khrushchev

Following the Walk, a group of walkers including Cyril and Regina had tea with Nina Khrushchev on 6 October 1961. Nina was the wife of Nikita Khrushchev Secretary General of the Communist Party of the USSR – the most powerful man in the USSR.

The article *"The San Francisco to Moscow Walk for Peace gets there"* concludes with tea with Mrs Khrushchev.

| Cyril | Regina | Mrs Khrushchev |

"The highlight of the Moscow visit... was our meeting with Mrs. Khrushchev on Friday October 6, at the Moscow House of Friendship...It had never occurred to me that it might be possible to meet her personally sometime, but when we were in Minsk on Friday September 22 I decided to take a chance and wrote to her. I addressed the letter to Mrs. Nina Khrushchev, Moscow, USSR, and did not really believe it would reach her or that anything would come of it.

To my surprise and delight after we got to Moscow we heard that Mrs. Khrushchev wanted to see us, especially the women. As we filled into the room of the House of Friendship we were surprised by her friendship and simplicity. No makeup, no Paris gown or foundation, just a dark dress, her hair in a simple style. She was friendly and plain, the kind of woman you would want to go to for encouragement and advice in something that was important.

Mrs. Khrushchev promised to tell her husband of the world's concern because of Soviet resumption of atomic bomb testing. At the same time she expressed concern over the necessity for such resumption...

Before we left, Mrs. Khrushchev gave us all little guide books illustrated with photographs of Moscow. One asked for her autograph and then all wanted it...

She told us, "The aim you have set yourselves is a most honourable one. My husband says "let us all drop our bombs into the ocean". I like that statement of his best of all. But we do not mean only our bombs when we say that but also those of other people. We have no alternative ..."

In addition to the article on the Walk, they also jointly wrote an article entitled **"We take tea with Mrs Khrushchev"** which was published in the magazine "Today" on December 2 1961. The account below is taken from that article.

"She wore no makeup. Her simple hair-do was loose at the back. Her dress was plain and modest. In fact she looked just like any matronly Russian family woman dressed in her Sunday best. But this was Mrs. Nina Khrushchev, wife of the leader of one-sixth of the world.

"You've had a lot of courage to do this," she told us - and suddenly our long, ten-month walk from California to Moscow seemed worth while.

There were eight of us altogether: six women and two men. We had been chosen to meet Mrs Khrushchev from among the thirty-one marchers who had marched halfway across the world in the course of peace." Cyril was one of the men.

The account continued;

"*We were ushered straight into a big, plushly decorated room with a long table in the centre. It was covered with apples in pedestal dishes, and paper wrapped chocolate candies.*

And standing next to it, with a warm friendly smile on her face, was Mrs. Khrushchev.

She looked the epitome of a grandmother - the sort of woman you know you can turn to for sympathy and advice.

There were only two other women with her: an interpreter and a woman who turned out to be a leader of the Soviet Peace Committee.

We walked up to Mrs. Khrushchev and introduced ourselves, shaking hands with her one by one. She spoke to each of us in a quiet, pleasant voice.

Then we all sat down around the table and took it in turns to tell her a bit about ourselves.

Mrs. Khrushchev listened to us quietly and asked questions through her interpreter.

She is a simple, charming woman, very impressive in her sincerity.

She wore no jewellery; her dress and jacket were made of a simple dark shot material; and her hair looked as though she had put it up herself, though we are sure she could have a hairdresser, every day if she wanted to.

All the time we were talking to her and telling her how important it was to prevent war we felt that she was completely in sympathy with us.

We are certain that she wasn't just listening for the sake of politeness - or diplomacy.

She kept interrupting and asking questions. If ever she disagreed she told us straight away.

After about twenty minutes the tea arrived. It was served in true Russian style, hot and black in glass beakers.

While we were drinking it we noticed how absolutely unpretentious this woman was.

She was very friendly all the time we were with her, and once she even spoke to us in good English.

When one of us appealed to her as a "mother" to try and stop all nuclear tests she replied quickly: "I am not only a mother but a grand-mother and a grand-grand-mother as well."

She disagreed when one of us suggested we should all follow Tolstoy's principles of non-violence.

"We do not follow those principles; these times are too complicated for that," she said in Russian.

"If only the politicians of all countries would unite in goodwill missions many problems would disappear."

We were only supposed to spend an hour with Mrs. Khrushchev. But when the time was up she looked down at her watch, smiled and said: "Oh, I think we should have another ten minutes. Tell me what happened to you on the way."

She was genuinely curious and we told her what happened in all the countries we marched through - especially about the warm reception the Russians had given us. It was time to go. We stood up and one of the boys took a few photographs of us with Mrs. Khrushchev.

She posed happily for the photographers and smiled at us as we stood in the bright sunlight streaming through the tall windows.

Just before we left she gave each of us autographed guide books of Moscow.

We told her we had three resolutions for 1962: to write a book about our march, to arrange a visit to America by several Russian women and to organise an American-Soviet chess match in New York.

"Women can help greatly toward peace," she said. "They are mothers and they know what suffering means. If it was up to women they would get rid of all armaments, I'm sure. Women should raise their hands against the war."

That was the end of our tea with Mrs. K. We don't think we converted her to our beliefs. But we are sure she sincerely wants peace in our world. Now she knows that a lot of other people throughout the world feel the same way. And perhaps this short, friendly woman, who doesn't look nearly as sophisticated as the room in which she received us, holds one of the keys to peace."

Regina is second from the left. You can just see Cyril's head poking out on the left of the picture below the chin of the woman standing

5

After the Walk

Regina Wender Fischer

Ella said that on the train on the way back from Moscow, Cyril proposed to Regina. Lynn Marsh, one of the walkers, remembers that as soon as they returned to London Cyril and Regina *"sort of went 'underground'"* and were difficult to reach. Karl heard later that they had travelled together in some East European countries, and then married and lived together in England. He said they were both very stubborn people and rather combative.

In addition to the article "We take tea with Mrs K" in "Today" was one on their romance.

THE ROAD TO ROMANCE

THE road to Moscow was tough at times for the thirty-one marchers who set out to walk to the Kremlin in the cause of peace. They were sometimes hungry, often weary, frequently abused.

But it was also a road to romance.

Six marchers were married by the time it was all over.

Regina Fischer, an American nurse, set out with the marchers from San Francisco in December last year. Four months later she was in London watching the Aldermaston marchers assemble in Trafalgar Square.

And among them was Cyril Pustan, a London plumber. He was handed a leaflet about the Moscow marchers—and at once decided to take part.

But it was not until the marchers were on the train back from Moscow that Cyril proposed to Regina. She accepted and they were married in London soon after their return.

There were two other marriages on the march. Both were American couples who had joined the party in the early stages.

Even if they didn't bring about world peace, there are three couples who reckon that the march achieved something.

Regina Fischer and Cyril Pustan who found romance on the march

Esther and Chaim were very much against the wedding and let Cyril know in no uncertain terms. However, they married on 20 October 1961 at Shoreditch Registry Office. Ella said that Chaim made sure they also had a wedding in the synagogue.

Regina was born in Switzerland on 31 March 1913 and was 16 years Cyril's senior. She moved as a small child to St Louis, and later moved to Mobile, Arizona, and then Brooklyn. She entered medical school in Moscow but dropped out in 1938 due to the onset of war, married a German biophysicist Gerhard Fischer, and moved back to the United States with him. They divorced when their children Joan and Bobby were 8 and 2 in Moscow, Idaho. Gerhardt dropped out of her life. She was always very active with a strong social conscience. She graduated as a nurse from New York University. She received an MA in 1958.

Brad Darrach wrote in *"Bobby Fischer vs the Rest of the World"* that Bobby was a chess prodigy, and she was very supportive of his career. She challenged the American Chess Federation over funding demanding an Inland Revenue Tax Audit when there were difficulties. She picketed the White House when the U.S. Department of State refused to give a student chess team permission to play in East Germany leading to a reversal in policy. Bobby hated this interference, and their relationship broke down when he was 15 and she left him to join the Peace March to Moscow. Ella told her granddaughter Samantha that Regina left Bobby as he was too moody, and he was on the border between genius and insanity. In December 1961, Bobby came to London to see Regina and Cyril for 10 days, and missed the US Chess Championship in doing so. It is thought to be the only occasion that Cyril met Bobby.

The chess world knew little about Cyril as Brad wrote that Cyril had Polish heritage (it was Ukrainian and German), was a Professor of English (he wasn't then), and they eventually settled in London (they never really did), and Harry Golombek wrote in *"The Inside Story of the World Chess Championship - Fischer v Spassky"* that Cyril had qualified as a Doctor of Medicine.

Cyril and Regina

An Englishman abroad - East Germany again – now working

In 1962 Cyril and Regina had a 2 week stay in Berlin after which they went some 165 miles south to Jena. Regina went to study. Cyril went to try and find work. Jena had a population of around 84,000 in 1964. It was a working-class city with a strong academic background. There were clashes between the academic elite and Nazi propogandists. Towards the end of World War II, it was heavily bombed by the American and British Allies. Jena fell within the Soviet zone of occupation in post-World War II Germany and became part of the GDR. In 1953, Jena was a centre of the East German Uprising against GDR policy. The protests with 30,000 participants drew fire from Soviet tanks. The following decades brought some radical shifts in city planning. During the 1960s when Cyril was living there, part of the historic city centre was demolished to build the Jena Tower.

Cyril told Ella that they were backed by the East German Government because of their involvement in the Moscow friendly Peace Walk and that Regina's costs were to be covered by Cyril. He said that applications for her to study elsewhere were rejected, and that Jena City Council was asked to provide them with an apartment. Cyril was awarded a job in the construction industry on 13 August 1962. They lived at 20 Brandstromster, Jena 69.

Cyril's 1971 CV notes that he worked as a fitter and welder at VEB Glaswerk Schott & Co in Jena from 1962 to 1963 full time, and from 1963 to 1964 part time. Part of the Schott factory had been dismantled and transported to the Soviet Union. Cyril's application for technical training in 1971, which he made while studying at Leeds University, stated that he also studied at the Institute of Welding in Halle for 2 days a week from October 1962 to January 1963.

Harald Wentzlaff-Eggebert opined in his article *"The FSU – a centre of espionage and brainwashing"* that Regina may

74

have chosen to study in East Germany for a number of reasons. Gerhardt Fischer was from East Berlin. Also, Bobby Fischer had been the top player in the US Chess team in the 1960 Chess Olympiad in Leipzig despite things being tense. It could also have been because Cyril had already produced 4 cassettes of an English textbook for an East German Publishing House, Volk and Wissen.

Harald noted that Cyril had produced a cassette of Robert Louis Stevenson's "the Bottle Imp" in 1948 for the Berliner Cornelsen Verlag, and 10 years later for Verlag Seven Seas Publishers "A Christmas Carol" by Charles Dickens. These later helped in his English lectures. Cyril continued this activity from Jena, because between 1962 and 1966 a series of 8 cassettes were published in Berlin, Leningrad, and Moscow especially for the blind spoken by Cyril in English.

In total they last for 15 ½ hours with Cyril's clear rich baritone voice adding depth to the written word. Youth by Conrad Joseph has been listened to by 32 people, A Christmas Carol in Prose by Charles Dickens by 39 people, The Lions Mane by Sir Arthur Conan Doyle by 46 people, Courage and other stories by John Galworthy by 21 people, The Bottle Imp by 31 people and

The Pavilion on the Sand Hills by 23 people both by Robert Louis Stevenson, and With Colt and Cocklebur short stories by O Henry by 28 people. They are still available at the German Central Library for the Blind.

The reason Cyril and Regina chose to live in East Germany was probably far simpler than Harald suggested. Ella said that Regina found difficulty getting into medical school in London due to her political views. To Cyril and Regina, East Germany was a Socialist/ Communist utopia created in the aftermath of World War II where the collective spirit as opposed to individual gain prevailed. The failure by the Communist Party in the United Kingdom to gain any political traction must have been dispiriting to Cyril. East Germany described itself as a *"workers and peasants state"* with a centrally planned economy and state ownership and governed by the Socialist Unity Party of Germany. It was supported by the USSR which had troops stationed there, fell within its orbit of control within the Warsaw Block, and supported other Marxist/ Socialist regimes and freedom movements throughout the world. The price of housing and basic goods and services were heavily subsidised and set by central government. There were often food shortages of items such as coffee and sugar in the period Cyril lived there, and its currency was weak internationally. Gender equality in East Germany may also have been a reason Regina wished to live there, it being further advanced and supported than in many Western countries.

Cyril will have seen the damaged buildings and pockmarked walls still providing evidence of the Allied bombing the state was unable to afford to repair given its weak economy. He will have noted the lack of advertising due to the lack of capitalist commercial activity. He will have experienced the egalitarian housing allocation.

Harald considered the theory that Regina was a Soviet spy who had been trained by Stalin in the 1930s, was active until the fall of the Berlin Wall on 9 November 1989, and was a member of the Stasi (the East German secret police).

Regina qualified as a Doctor on 29 December 1964 at the Friedrich-Schiller University and worked in Jena until 1971. She was single minded in pursuit of her education and professional life, and despite her radical lifestyle may simply not have had the time or energy to be of much use as a spy in a town in the very south of East Germany.

Welding

Cyril wrote in GDR Review in edition 5 of 1966 in his article *"A new Job with a Difference"* that;

"The floor is hard but comfortable as long as I don't lie on a loose nut or bolt. Through the dark hue of welding goggles, the intensely hot oxyacetylene flame looks tame enough to pat, but don't try it. Everything has a subdued colour. Mechanically, the motions are repeated: keep a molten pool, push the welding rod into the pool between the joint, fuse it into the pool, get an even buildup of thickness and continue. Rod and pipe flow together into an even rippled patterned joint. How easy overhead welding is! Flame control, and there's nothing to it!

Nothing to it? I remember the beginning - burnt fingers, cascades of sparks cunningly sneaking through the most securely buttoned clothes and nestling against the skin of the chest, and the acrid smell of smouldering cloth with a concomitant feeling of hotness, signifying that your shirt, overall jacket, or trousers, or sometimes all three, were burning.

Those are forgotten days. Now I lie uncomfortably comfortable, weld without conscious effort, and dream the dreams which a wandering mind can conjure up in its imagination. Or sometimes I think back on how I got started on this episode of my life. It began bang in the middle of August, 1962, when after a two-week stay in Berlin, my wife and I left for a university town in the GDR, she to study and I to win the bread. This is what is commonly known as a good working arrangement.

I went to the local employment office. There was one small problem - I could not speak, read or write a single word of German and could barely understand just a very few words. Nevertheless, I was undaunted. My wife had assured me a week or two in a factory was all that was needed to learn the language, and in two to three months I should have a fluent command of German. I guess I was a born sucker.

I played with the idea of asking for a job as a roadsweeper or maybe going up in the world and becoming a chimney sweep. In this way I could work on my own and avoid many of the daily contacts that might prove an embarrassment when finding myself unable to participate in everyday chitchat.

Having for several years worked in the building industry, I said to myself: "Maybe I'll work on a building site again." The woman in charge of the employment office obligingly rang up someone or other who made a special trip over. He looked at me, said: "No German? Impossible! Unthinkable!" So a second phone call and over came someone else from another building site. He thought I might earn more in a factory and again that the language might be a problem. Five faces enquiringly turned in my direction, each pair of eyes silently asking: "Well, what are you going to do?" What should I do?

My thoughts returned to the idea of a factory. A third phone call, over came the personnel officer from one of the biggest factories in town. The situation was explained to him. I was glad my wife had come with me to act as interpreter, otherwise no explaining could have been done. Among the several sections of this factory was a power and steam producing plant which not only supplied the factory with heat and electricity but piped both these products to other factories in the area. The maintenance staff in this section received a fairly high rate of pay because the work called for a high degree of skill, was heavy, and also at times dirty and dangerous. Each of these items involved additional payment.

It was suggested that I work in this department. We went there. The engineer in charge took us around. It was a strange new world. Pipes of all dimensions, some big enough for a man to get lost in, were coming from all directions and going in all directions. Some were lagged, some painted green, some painted red, many not painted at all. Here a drip of escaped water, there a wisp of condensed steam, big cylinders, water valves, steam valves, water gauges, steam gauges, low pressure gauges, high pressure gauges, more and more pipes, more and more valves, pumps and noise!

Suddenly the flange packing on a large steam valve blew out. It sounded as if a steam train had rushed madly into the boiler house, screaming, hissing, panting like a wild untamed monster from the legends of mythology. Large white clouds of condensed vapour appeared as the steam spewed forth with deafening shrill discord, like half the factory sirens in London going together. I waited fearfully the expected crescendo when all would shatter in a tumultuous explosion. It never happened. The uproar came no nearer, it didn't recede, but just galloped crazily on and on, like an express going through a tunnel at full speed and never emerging. I saw the engineer's lips moving but heard nothing. His voice was greedily swallowed by the surrounding din. If I worked in this hubbub there wouldn't be much conversation and I'd make sure my ears were well stuffed with cotton wool.

The engineer made for the trouble spot. Men were moving quickly along the cat-walks overhead to attend to this emergency, and when the big hand wheel had been turned and turned and the valve finally closed, the sound receded to a low continuous puffing.

Adjoining the boiler house was on oxygen producing plant. Here was comparative quietness and coolness. Over the steady hum of the compressors the engineer's voice was once more audible. He thought it advisable before I made a decision that I visit other sections of the factory so that I could decide for myself which

I thought would suit me best. I looked around the rest of the factory and decided that I would settle to work in the boiler house.

I had never worked in the boiler house of a factory before. It would be something new, interesting, even challenging. The sceptics say: "So what!", and the pessimists say: "What for? In the end you'll finish up 6 feet under and then how far will all your experience have got you!" Rubbish, how wrong they are! A new venture is life renewed. Basically as yet the whole world lies undiscovered, and in this old world I was for myself entering into a new one.

Everything was fixed up. The following Monday I was to begin, but first there would have to be a medical examination. This is a must in the GDR for everyone starting a new job anywhere. I discovered, too, that industrial workers have an annual checkup. Also should you prove unfit for a heavy job, a light job must be found for you, all factories being obligated to employ a percentage of disabled labour.

The factory, like most, had its own emergency station, dental surgery, creche, kindergarten, and clinic. It was to this clinic I went for my checkup. I was fluoroscoped, bled and dewatered. A lady doctor tapped and thumped me without ill effect.

On Monday I reported to work, in one hand a paper bag with a new pair of work boots I had bought the previous Saturday, in the other hand a couple of wrapped up cheese sandwiches. I walked through the gate accompanied by my wife. The seven-thirty hooter sounded. First I had to go to the various offices, fill in a biography, present photographs, pick up a factory pass and so on, then down to my work section and into the engineer's office. On my pass they had entered me down as a stoker's mate, but when the engineer saw the pass he said that this was wrong, as I was going to be employed as a skilled worker, namely a "Reparaturschlosser". What is a Schlosser? I still don't really know. The dictionary says a locksmith, but I am no locksmith. Later on several occasions I saw workpeople making keys for themselves, but they were no locksmiths either. I guess a fitter would be the nearest English equivalent.

One of the fellows in the office spoke some English. He had had six years of it at school and then been a British prisoner of war in Italy, where he said he had managed to get some English practice. He greeted us with: "How do you do?" Then I was introduced to the charge hand, known here as the "brigadier". He is in charge of a team or a gang of workmen. He was a short stocky fellow about forty, with a slight limp, receding hairline, and a friendly manner. We shook hands. Formalities over, my wife left. Through the office window I saw her walk down the road towards the gate. Now I was on my own.

I saw too some of the hills around the town. One high hill formed a fine background, fresh and green and gold in the morning sun. I have since seen it covered in snow, have climbed it and stood on the plateau on the First of May after the big parade in the town. The early summer flowers were just beginning to bloom then and the wind on its peak was still blowing gusty and strong. There are other hills surrounding the town but this one has found a permanent place in my memory."

He left Schott and Co on 25 May 1963.

From June to October 1963 he worked as a welder for VEB Rohrleitungsbau in Berlin on Hans-Loch-Strasse where the foreman wrote that *"his work discipline can be described as exemplary...but it has to be said that Mr Pustan has some difficulties regarding the German language – however these did not affect his work performance."*

He returned to Schott and Co on 14 October 1963 to work as a fitter in the power plant.

Mr Hirsch wrote on 30 May 1964 that he *"brought a lot of energy and ambition to hand over his work in a qualitative manner...and his attitude towards work was exemplary"* which was why on 1 May 1964 he was honoured by Schott and Co for being the best worker and given a bonus of 50 DDR Marks.

Victor remembers that the workers there, finding Cyril was a very pro-GDR left winger, made clear to Cyril that they wanted no admonitions about their customary listening to West Berlin radio during work. Most regularly heard was RIAS – Radio in American Sector – a joint enterprise with the CIA, and Victor Grossman thinks this surprised Cyril, at least at the beginning.

In his article *"A new Job with a Difference"* Cyril wrote in GDR Review 7/66;

"Here I was standing in the office of a publicly-owned factory, the former big shots of nazi times gone for good. This engineer took a bottle of milk out of his brief case, drank from the bottle and bit on a sandwich, and told the team leader to look after me. The engineer was a decent fellow, firm but fair and approachable. He had the common touch about him.

I followed him to the office he shared with the foreman, or Meister, as they call them in the GDR. I was given new work clothes, jacket, trousers, shirt, a towel, and a bar of soap. The work clothes would be laundered weekly by the factory free of charge. Although the clothes had numbers on them, sometimes mix-ups occurred. One Monday one of the tallest fitters came into the workshop wearing what looked like a pair of overall shorts, while I had on a pair of work trousers turned up six times. There was a burst of laughter at the sight of his bare hairy legs. We swapped togs and put the matter right then and there.

After I was given my work clothes I had to have a locker, so we went to a locker room behind the oxygen producing plant. This was a small room with accommodation for about ten people. Beside the lockers, the room had a shower, washbasin, toilet,

82

chairs and a table - it was the changing room for the shift workers in the oxygen plant. There were two of them, one for work clothes and one for my other clothes.

The team leader was waiting outside for me. He took me to the workshop, gave me a sandwich from his briefcase, and said he would be back soon. I stood around waiting. In between times various members of the team came in, shook hands and greeted me. The team leader came back with a piece of pipe in his hand, welded a stop end on, and then hurried out again. I must hand it to him he was a good craftsman and a fine welder. I later learned that he had been a wartime pilot.

Then someone else came in, his arms loaded with bottles of milk which he deposited in various work places. He handed me one too. I assumed he knew what he was doing so I took it. It was impossible to understand a word he was saying to me. It was German plus a local dialect. But by his actions it was obvious he wanted the empty bottle back again. I learned later that a pint of milk is distributed free every other day to all heavy workers or workers engaged in jobs with health hazards, such as dust, fumes, smoke, heat, etc.

At quarter to twelve the first lunch hooter went off. I thought of sitting down somewhere to eat my cheese sandwiches for lunch. But the team leader came back and took me to the canteen. It was a big hall where several hundred people were eating a hot meal. I tried the diet meal and found that it was not intended for vegetarians, and so left it uneaten. This was all subsequently taken care of when I was later called into the engineer's office. There sat the engineer, the canteen manager, the brigadier, the trade union secretary, and one of the factory research scientists who knew some English and had come to act as interpreter.

The trade union secretary spoke first and told me there were a number of safety regulations I would have to observe. "Firstly, no sleeping in the boilers." I chuckled to myself. How could anyone be able to enter a flaming hot boiler, let alone sleep there? But some time later when working in a boiler that had been shut down for repairs, I thought I had discovered a corpse. It was only one of the fellows comfortably stretched out on some big paper bags to keep his clothes clean, fast asleep. Then I realized how dangerous this was. He could be burned or asphyxiated in his sleep if the boiler fires were relit.

"Secondly, no smoking in the oxygen plant." I said I didn't smoke, and in any case no sensible person would smoke near oxygen. The secretary said he was glad to hear I was sensible but in the GDR law requires that a worker is officially informed of safety regulations.

"Thirdly,..." and he went on through the list.

The next question was the question of food. The interpreter was lost for words. This was outside his field of research. "Do you eat Kartoffeln, Kartoffeln, K-A-R...," and he thumbed through his dictionary. "Aha, aha, I have it, potatoes!" "Yes".

"Do you eat -let me see. When I was a POW in England I had Haferlocken, Haferlocken..." He licked his finger and turned the pages. Flick, flick, flick. "H-A-F, aha, aha, I have it. " He gave a triumphant squeak. "Porridge!" "Do you eat porridge?" "I don't mind porridge." So on it went.

I had been duly informed of the safety regulations, my diet had been sorted out, my wage group had been decided on. I was set for a while.

The factory, it turned out, had two canteens, a large one and a small one for people on special diets ordered by medical advice. The meals in both canteens cost about a quarter of what it would cost in a restaurant, being subsidized by the plant trade union.

Once more back to the workshop. On the team leader's face was a puzzled frown as he turned the pages of his notebook, figuring what he could give me to do. It was no good him looking at me because I certainly couldn't help him. "Come with me," he said, and took me around the place. He opened one of the small observation doors of the biggest boiler. The whole interior was glowing red hot, so bright it hurt the eyes. he pointed and said, "Feuer," then indicating the large tubes said "Dampf," and then taking me to the turbine said, "Strom." I had the whole story first, steam, turbine, electricity. Simple, yet not so simple.

Then he thought of something for me to do. A new piece of one-inch tubing had to be fitted somewhere. He showed me the job, showed me where the new tubing was kept, got out a pair of ratchet stocks and dies, gave me a screwdriver, pipe wrench, pliers, hacksaw, a two-meter wooden rule, and that was it. I went back to the job and looked it over. Then I measured the pipe. Strange to be measuring something in meters, centimeters, and millimeters, while you are mentally trying to visualise it in feet and inches. The pipe sizes were standard English sizes. Thank goodness, something was familiar. Happy at having a job to do, I cut up the pipe, threaded the pieces, and screwed them together.

One or two of the team coming into the shop to pick up a tool or a fitting or to have a swig of lemonade or coffee said I was working too hard. They wanted to know what my trade or profession was, was I a Schlosser? I got the impression everybody was a Schlosser, or a Heizer, or a Meister or something or other. Not one of them considered himself a nothing and nobody thought anybody else was better than himself. One of them, a young fellow of about 24, told me that from tomorrow he and I would be working together. "I'll teach you German and you teach me English."

Having finished the job I went back to the shop for some more work. It was two o'clock. The team leader said "Feierabend," which meant in plain language it was knocking off time, and told me that tomorrow I should come in at six. The team made an early start in the summer months. Some came from long distances, others worked on their allotment gardens, raised small livestock or did odd jobs.

I walked to the changing room across the open yardway, past the big cooling towers, the oxygen storage tanks, the factory locomotives and the trucks. I heard the whirr of the activity that is the throbbing pulse of every factory, composed of the music of machine power and human endeavor that swells and surges proudly, and so it should. Its melody is devised by men, it is conducted by men, and when good men take this wonder of their own creation into their own hands it enriches the lives of all.

I showered and changed, then walked down one of the factory roads, hoping not to get lost. I saw a string of glass furnaces through the open doors of the glass shop, where glass blowers with their blow pipes were giving shape and form to cherry red masses of molten glass. Many a craft and trade requires as much intelligence, application and skill to master as most of the professions. Indeed the capability of many craftsman is such that they would learn a profession far more quickly than they learnt their trade.

Man needs other things beside everyday work in order to live a fuller life. Owing to the language difficulties several months elapsed before I discovered that the factory catered for this need and had many cultural and hobby groups. A six-foot high noticeboard near the main gate announced the day and time each group met; art, drama, band, chess, choir, film making, football, photography, piano accordion, sewing, stamp collecting, and so on. The factory also ran its own trade school and provided special training for workers who desired it. There were tailoring, dressmaking, and boot repair workshops, a library, a branch bank, a grocery shop, etc., all within the factory.

Near the gate I saw several of my new workmates from the team. How different people look when the dust of industry has been washed off, when the oil smears have been removed, and they wear different clothes. It is a complete transfiguration. I passed through the gate, remembering to show my pass. Walking down the sloping road to the center of the town, still holding my cheese sandwiches, I was aware that I had not in the true sense of the word earned my pay that day. But this had been no ordinary day. For the first time I had worked in a factory owned by people and not by private bosses, and it felt good. My first day at my new job was over."

Teaching

Whilst working, Cyril was asked to teach a few English classes at Humboldt University in Berlin in 1963 where Dr Hansen wrote on 19 July 1963 *"In the final evaluation, the language courses of Mr. Pustan were very much loved by all participants because they were varied and lively."*

Lutz Hummel attended a number of Cyril's lectures. He said that Cyril and Regina were considered to be an unusual couple for a number of reasons. They were the only people from the "Free World" to live in Jena. Regina was obviously much older than Cyril. Regina dressed very scruffily unlike the screen depiction of American women, something she also did when she was in London, and Cyril while tidy did not have the look of an English gentleman and wore old fashioned clothes. Lutz thought the reason the authorities were so keen for Cyril to teach English, and in particular at the Friedrich-Schiller University in Jena, was because it was so unusual to have an English person living in East Germany given its poor economic position and lack of freedoms. Their uniqueness made them well known at the University. He never heard Cyril speak German as all his classes were in English and everyone spoke to him in English. He played a guitar in classes and used folk songs. He knew that Cyril went on demonstrations, but they never discussed politics. He knew that Cyril was active in the Peace Movement and had been on the 1961 Peace March. Cyril was known to be an honourable man of good character who was thought to be naïve, and in some respects simple, due to his support for the Soviet regime that was so hated by East Germans.

Victor remembers that Cyril was not unhappy at his teaching job and felt that some teachers were not very left wing, and others were very right wing.

Cyril gave 2 hours of lectures a week at the Friedrich-Schiller University on English Conversation in April 1963 for which he was paid 10 DDR Marks per week. He became an assistant lecturer at the Friedrich-Schiller University in April 1964 initially on a 6-month maternity cover contract with a monthly salary of 850 DDR Marks and 24 days annual leave. This was extended and his salary increased to 950 DDR Marks, by 1969 was 1,010 DDR Marks, by 1973 was 1,015 DDR Marks, and from 1975 to 1977 was 1,090 DDR Marks. This, according to Lutz, was a relatively good income when compared to the average.

Cyril's classes were with scientists but then extended to medical lecturers.

Victor remembers that when he and his wife Renate had Cyril round for a meal once in Berlin, they fretted over what to feed him as he was a vegan. They eventually gave him lettuce and tomatoes which he was very pleased with. He remembers that Cyril did not look underfed or skinny and was strong. Veganism was not as widespread or known about during Cyril's adult life. In 1944, the term was used for the first time, and Donald Watson published the first newsletter in the United Kingdom, called "Vegan News". It was associated most often with Buddhism, Hinduism, and Jainism which had virtually no community in the United Kingdom or East Germany in this period. It was not part of the Ashkenazi Jewish tradition which Cyril had been brought up in – a tradition that had staples such as chicken soup, stews, salt beef, and chopped and fried fish. Cyril was a food anomaly in the Jewish world. There was not even a Jewish Vegetarian Society in the United Kingdom until the 1960's.

In his application to renew his residence card in East Germany in 1964 Cyril wrote;

"I would like my stay in the DDR...to be extended. Firstly I want to study German, then a natural science subject, because that increases my teaching activity enormously since I mainly teach natural scientists. If the former is not possible I would have liked to study English and American literature. My expected stay here is for at least five years."

Cyril wrote articles in Volkswacht *"The magnificent strides"* on 18 May 1965, in Junge Welt on *"Unrest in the boat of the Labour Party"* on 13 October 1965 and *"A bus drive through England"* on 15 October 1965, and in Fur Dich on *"Demonstration against rent increases"* on 1 December 1965.

Cyril wrote about a course he taught on from 12 September 1966 to 6 October 1966;

"From the 12th of September to 6th of October - twenty four days and only one of them rainy. For the rest it was dark skies and blue nights. From my room window I saw the black slated rooftops and the slate hung walls of the village houses blend with the trees and the rolling downs of the surrounding countryside. 850 metres above sea level was like being on top of the world. For a few minutes I stood at my casement admiring the soft moonlit splendour. But work had to be done, so I pulled the curtains and settled down to finish preparing the next day's work. From the room opposite I heard the plodding tap-tap-tap of unseeing fingers groping for the right typewriter key. From down the passageway I could hear the tappity-tappity-tappity-tap of other fingers which were obviously much practised in finding the right key. Thus I heard and knew other teachers too were doing their homework. The thin partition wall of the room vibrated to the rhythmic snores of my next door neighbour - sleep deeply dear friend. It's near the hour of midnight. Besides, it's better you sleep soundly now, in your bed, than tomorrow in my class.

In the grey of dawn the curtains were again opened. Sometimes the white, misty, vapoury clouds too were still sleeping, their hazy forms lazily draped across mother earth. And then the early sun rose, reached out with its ninety two million mile long arms, and gently lifted the clouds aloft to reveal the lush green carpet of meadow enjoying the late September and early October Indian summer.

The proud upright trees in the wooded backgrounds, the weather, the scenery, the general atmosphere, suited and were in harmony with the occasion. For in the far off region of Masserberg - if you do not consider Masserberg a far off region, I must explain that the centre of my world is the Holmarkt; and anywhere beyond there is, as far as I am concerned, a far off region.

Jena was making history. Ten "students" were taking part in the first ever intensive English course conducted by the Abteilung Sprachunterricht Jena.

They were not students in the ordinary sense of the word. For one thing, they were a little older, mostly in their thirties. They came from various walks of university life: law, medicine, psychology, philosophy, agriculture, chemistry, and physics. Their levels of knowledge varied, but all who took part in the course did so with the intention of working. And work it was from morn till night. Work for the students and work for the teachers.

From 8:30 a.m. onwards it was English all the way, the main emphasis being on the spoken language...

What were the topics covered in the classes?

A. Modern Britain, a survey of life, customs, and habits in Britain today.

B. "Meet the Robinsons" a lively text about a British engineer living in the Soviet Union who takes his Russian born wife on a holiday trip to England. This text introduced the students to modern idiomatic English. At first the students found the book heavy going, but soon it became a favourite with them, and they were sorry to leave the last few chapters unfinished.

C. A specially prepared series of ten minute lessons on slides, with accompanying tape recordings, covering various topics, including the mystery of Salomon Grundy and the search for him by Inspector Curlilocks Bones from the "Yard".

D. There was a good coverage of English grammar, which was well presented in its various aspects.

E. Songs, a total of nearly thirty English and American folk and working class songs were taught. In this connexion a book has been prepared by the Abteilung Sprachunterricht Jena, the first book of its kind in the GDR. It is hoped to prepare a second such booklet which will contain up to 50 or more songs.

F. An outline was given of the British Universities, the Royal Society of London, and so on.

This wasn't all. Several very enjoyable afternoons were spent walking in the lovely surroundings of Masserberg. And while walking, most of the participants conducted their conversation entirely in English, using the opportunity to ask many questions and discuss practically every topic under the sun.

The television programme "English for you" was seen and all were advised to continue this practise in the future. I personally found the programme an excellent way of studying English and am willing to volunteer one evening a month reviewing and practising the material of the television course with all those learning English. Especially, to help them with the intonation and pronunciation.

Some evenings the participants had to themselves to continue their private study and then maybe have a quiet pint or two in the local.

On a number of other evenings, about twelve in all, a sixty to ninety minute programme was arranged after supper. Slides of London, Cambridge, and other places in Britain were shown and discussed. English and American folk and popular songs were learnt and lustily sung. Vocabulary building, and quiz games were played. Two lively evenings were spent discussing conditions in Britain. A very interesting evening was spent discussing the 13th Party Plenum. An evening was spent listening to hits from "My Fair Lady".

All in all, a full schedule and I haven't mentioned everything - the list would be too long, but I'll add two more things: all of the above mentioned activities as well as practically everything else we did was conducted ENTIRELY IN ENGLISH, even during dinner and supper at our table the conversation was entirely in English.

An intensive language course means that you speak and speak and speak the language. That is what the participants did. Some could be heard learning the vocabulary at six o'clock in the morning, others at eleven o'clock at night.

To the four teachers working with the group it was heartening to hear the daily progress made by the participants. These courses are of course strenuous for the student. They are also strenuous for the teacher. To show their appreciation the students gave their teachers an evening out.

Looking back on the past three and a half weeks, reflecting on the praise and the criticisms of the participants, it can be emphatically said that the course was a success, and that the second one will still be more successful.

By popular request the first course did not end at Masserberg as planned. The participants want to continue with their grammar, to learn more songs, and to again "Meet the Robinsons". To do this they are going to meet one evening a week during the next term.

To the organisers and teachers of the course the greatest reward was the tangible improvement in the standard of English of all the participants. This compensated for the late nights, the hours and hours of preparation and everything else that was put into the first intensive teaching course carried out by the Abteilung Sprachunterricht Jena."

Victor took part in special English Improvement courses for scientists working in the many research institutes of the GDR Academy of Sciences. Cyril told Victor some of the language tricks and games he used to get his students to speak more fluently. Victor tried a few of them including the idea of debates – pro and con, conducted with rules like those in a high school debating club.

In his undated essay *"Jan in Jena"*, Cyril writes about a worker's journey on the tram and identifies stops which he may well have used, and which Lutz Hummel confirmed exist. The route taken was Steinborn, Breite Strasse, over the Camsdorfer Bridge which spanned the Saale River, through the Thaelmann Ring, and on to Holzmarkt where people alighted for Schott's and the University. Having alighted Jan walked past the Psychological Chemical Institute, past the "Max Reger" music shop, the newly built Zeiss skyscraper, detoured around Westbahnhof Strasse, past the post office, the Biology Institute, past Schiller House and back to Westbahahof Strasse.

On 12 September 1966 Dr Friedrich Beer wrote *"as a working class child Mr Pustan clearly recognised the great advantages of our social order and understood it excellently from his own experience...His hard work, extraordinary willingness to help, humility, his political attitude and his great expertise have earned him the respect and recognition of the entire team."*

Dr Beer noted on 13 April 1967 that *"his political stance is very progressive, which is expressed, among other things, in his clear position of the dirty war of the USA in Vietnam (he donated for example over 600 deutschmarks to solidarity for Vietnam). Several times he took to the press to explain his political position."*

From 1967 to 1970 he studied for and was awarded the equivalent of a BA and then an MA in English and Education with modules in Psychology, Pedagogics, and Methodology at the Friedrich-Schiller University.

Professor Geyer of the University wrote on 4 October 1971 that Cyril;

"has been working as a teacher of English for almost ten years at our institute. During this time he gave weekly lessons of 2 hours duration for a group of about 5-10 scientists, and additional lessons of identical length for the head of the institute. Mr. Pustan's lessons were built up logically in spite of the differing levels of knowledge of the participants, which he always took into consideration. Therefore, he provided the members of the class with an increasing knowledge and ability of using the English language. These results were gained by a lively kind of teaching and by many innovations, for instance his own audio-visual material which made it easy to get his participants involved. His teaching was enhanced by a profound knowledge and understanding of medical terminology.

For all of this I wish to express my deepest gratitude to Mr. Pustan, for his tireless efforts and all his kindness during this time on behalf of my staff and myself."

This was just part of his teaching programme some of which in 1974 and 1975 was aimed at Soviet interpreters which Professor

Leitel noted on 7 May 1975 included *"the preparation of always up to date teaching material based on an in depth study of the English progressive newspapers ("Morning Star", "Marxism Today", "New York Times" and others)."*

Cyril was thanked for his work by the Ministry of Higher and Technical Education of the Council of Ministers of East Germany on 17 September 1974.

Dr Friedrich Beer wrote;

"Our initial concern that Mr Pustan as a non-philologist and because of his relatively incomplete school education could not fully meet the requirements, have proven to be unfounded. It turned out that Mr Pustan had acquired a very good general knowledge. He conducts his lessons with great love, he prepares himself very carefully and methodically, and he has made significant progress. In the classroom he gave the listener additional literature from the "Daily Worker" with specific English problems, and he had interesting discussions for example about the high rents and low pensions in the UK. He is extremely familiar with the problems of English Unions and the Communist Party of Great Britain.

He is very open to our social order, he regularly takes part in the department events, although he does not take part in public discussions due to language difficulties. For a year now, however, he had been attending a German course for foreigners on a regular basis and has already made some progress, particularly with regard to understanding.

He is extremely modest and reserved in his demeanour, and it is difficult for him to come into contact with strangers. It takes a long acquaintance before he goes out a little more. In his personal life he is obviously completely under the influence of his wife, his further perspectives depend also essentially on where his wife will turn to after completing her studies.

The head of the English editing department, General Hahn, informed me that of all the English people he knows here in the German Democratic Republic, he has the best impression of Mr Pustan and that he would urgently support him because of his achievements so far..."

Acting and Films

In 1967, he played the Chief of Staff of the Royal Air Force in the DEFA film "Die gefrorenen Blitze - The Frozen Lightening" by Janos Veiczi – the irony being that he was a lifelong Pacifist. The film was about the British consulate in Norway receiving documents saying that the Nazis were conducting secret rocket research in Peenumunde. The British doubted the authenticity of the so called "Oslo report". The experiments continued unimpeded. Resistance fighters tried to sabotage the base. When the first "V2" rocket was successfully launched, the Allied commanders finally become interested in the "Oslo report".

Victor was also in the film and remembers that the director wanted native English speakers. He organised a taxi to bring Cyril from Jena to where they were filming in Potsdam-Babelsberg, a distance of 150 miles. When he got there and the English speakers were given their lines, Cyril had not got one, so they all spoke to the Director who rewrote the act and gave Cyril a line. He is credited with this acting role through IMDb despite only appearing in the first scene and unfortunately, it appearing that his line cut in the editing process of the film. Cyril was paid 75 DDR Marks for his day's work. Victor noted that Cyril did not really look like the director's perception of an English gentleman presumably due to his Eastern European roots.

John Green who also appeared in the film remembered Cyril as *"a rather quiet and modest man who played his part without any fuss or ado."* Cyril looked smart and the part, if a little young – he was 38.

Cyril on the far right as the Chief of Staff of the RAF

This was not the only time Cyril appeared on a film credit. He was played by Shawn Campbell in the 2014 biopic of Bobby Fischer's series of matches against the Soviet chess Grandmasters culminating in the 1972 match with Boris Spassky, Pawn Sacrifice. The depiction of Cyril had significant artistic license. According to the film Cyril and Regina were living together in Brooklyn in October 1959 even though they did not meet until 1961 and Cyril never visited the United States. Still at least Shawn had a speaking part. In the first scene in which he appears, Bobby comes back to their apartment in Brooklyn from having won a chess tournament, complains about the noise, and rails against Regina's lifestyle and association with communists. When Cyril and Regina emerge from her bedroom in Brooklyn, with Cyril in his vest and underpants and saying the immortal line "Bobby" (that being his only spoken part in the film), Bobby calls him "size twelves" as he holds Cyril's shoes in disgust and demands that Regina left. Cyril only appears once more in the background in the flat with Regina when Bobby beats Boris in the seminal 6th game. Tobey Maguire played Bobby, Leif Schreiber played Boris, Robin Weigert played Regina, and Lily Rabe played Joan, Bobby's sister.

Music

Ella said Cyril wanted to sing. He played the guitar.

He also had a large collection of records, Gilbert and Sullivan songbooks, and Folk Song books some of which he owned with Ella who shared his passion for music and formed the basis for his later use of Folk Songs in his academic life. His record collection comprised some 140 vinyl records of which 60 were Paul Robeson double A side songs. His collection was mainly of folk and workers songs but also included Yiddish, Jewish prayers, classical, Big Band, and some "Teach yourself Russian" records.

Some of his music books

Cyril and Regina had become friends with Christine Patzer, and in her letters to Ella she wrote;

"Cyril often helped me when I was given a difficult translation to do. I have not forgotten his kindness." She also wrote *"I am sending you a number of picture postcards collected by Cyril. We used them in our classes for background teaching. The students were always very interested in the sights of England. From many of the picture-postcards Cyril and Regina made slides."*

Other activities

Cyril maintained regular contact with family in London. On 9 August 1966, he wrote offering sympathy on hearing of Chaim's ill-health and recent operation. He referred to his own health saying;

"I can still feel the bang I got on the back of my head, and for several months I had dizzy spells as a result of the bang. I went to see the neurologist at the clinic – he attends one of my classes – who told me that this is a general condition following an injury and generally gets better, but it takes time."

He then told them about upcoming teaching commitments in Leipzig and Jena and to write to him at home as;

"I don't go to the university department every day."

Posters advertising his talks in Berlin in 1968 and 1969

Cyril lived through a tumultuous period of world history in the 1960's in East Germany. This included the Cuban missile crisis, the assassinations of President Kennedy Senator Bobby Kennedy and Martin Luther King, the escalation of the Vietnam War, the rise of the Civil Rights movement in the USA, the fight against Apartheid in South Africa, the independence of many former Western colonies such as Kenya, the fall of Nikita Khrushchev, the formation of Harold Wilson's Labour Government, the Maoist Cultural Revolution in China that led to the persecution of millions, the 6 day war in 1967 between Israel and Egypt Syria and Jordan, the crushing of the pro-democracy uprising in Czechoslovakia by Soviet troops, and the space race between the USA and USSR culminating in the Moon landing.

Cyril was a member of the German-Soviet Friendship Society from 1966 to 1972. This was an organisation set up by the East German government in 1949 to encourage closer cooperation with the Soviet Union. In addition to political agitation, it organised numerous sports and cultural events where the main topic was socialising and getting to know a different culture than ones' own.

Cyril and Regina attended the 8th World Peace Congress in East Berlin in June 1969 *"which was widely criticized by various participants for its lack of spontaneity and carefully orchestrated Soviet supervision"* according to the United States Department of State Foreign Affairs Note of April 1985.

Cyril also attended the 20th Anniversary celebrations of the DDR upon which he later gave slide talks, as well as the World Youth Festival in Berlin in 1973. This was the 3rd time he had been to the Festival. There were 25,000 participants from all over the world joining some 700,000 East German youth and guests who attended. As with the earlier Festivals he attended in 1955 and 1957, there were parades, music, dancing, art exhibitions, sports events, and political seminars lasting 9 days. It was known colloquially as the Red Woodstock and the motto was *"Anti-imperialist solidarity, peace, and friendship"*.

Relaxing in the countryside

The synthesis of his political philosophy, teaching, and love of music

From 1967 to 1970 Cyril completed a degree in English and American Studies and published his thesis the *"Role of Folk Song in Teaching Foreign Languages"* at Jena on 20 April 1969. In the introduction to his 105-page manuscript he wrote;

"Folk songs have three basic uses in teaching foreign languages - they help in teaching the language itself (language study) - they are useful aids for acquiring information about and insights into the cultural background of the countries whose language is being learned - they are powerful weapons which are of aid to progressive people the world over in the battle of ideas ...

To explain how I came to realise the need for teaching singing to GDR English classes takes me back to the year 1963 when I was asked to give a few English lessons at Humboldt University. The class was to consist of teachers of English taking a brief summer refresher course. I planned my programme for the week and included in it a number of British and American folksongs because, I felt, folk songs express something that is typically native, and they express it in a way which cannot easily be conveyed by any other medium. I had no song books nor were any obtainable. Time was short, so I had copies of the words of the songs I wished to teach duplicated. I did not know how the few minutes I had allocated for those songs in my timetable would be received by the teachers. To my surprise their knowledge of English songs was rather scanty. "My Bonnie" seemed to be about the only song they all knew. It was soon clear they needed and wanted more, so every day we sang for 15 minutes. Since then I have included songs as part of the English lesson and have always found them to be appreciated."

He continued;

"In folk songs language teachers have a valuable aid given to them, in a manner of speaking, on a silver platter. Folk song lends warmth and colour to the otherwise often rather prosaic, matter-of-fact classroom atmosphere. The resultant emotional charge not only heightens the intensity of foreign language learning, but carries over into other subjects as well."

He recalls his working life;

"While working in a factory in Jena and on building sites in Berlin I have had workers and office employees come up and tell me that they had learned English twenty or thirty years ago at school. Through lack of practice they had forgotten practically every word they had learned. Painfully, they would try to recall a word or two, but without success. Then without warning, they would burst out with "My Bonnie" or "She'll be Coming Round the Mountain" or some other song. The tune was correct, the words flowed freely, the pleasure was still undiminished. A song is something that stays with you. The advertising jingles on radio and television have become inescapable and all-pervading in Britain and America for exactly this reason."

He writes about how folk songs promote solidarity saying;

"Songs have long been recognised as weapons which can be used by progressive people to help win the battle of ideas. Songs are an indispensable part of strikes, peace demonstrations and protest actions in Britain and America. Folk song concerts at large concert halls ... are not only unforgettable cultural events but serve as rallying centres and sources of inspiration. People go from them strengthened in their determination to do their share in the cause of the progressive movement.

Songs open all the outpourings of human emotion to us. They bring home to us the essential oneness of the human race and the identity between the common people of all nations and races... Among the worst effects of the present political situation are the barriers which Britain and especially America set up during the cold war to prevent or minimise contact between performing artists and audiences in their countries, on the one hand, and the socialist countries on the other.

On the comparatively few occasions when Russian folk singers were able to sing in Britain or America, they aroused universal admiration for their amazing talent and artistry. Interestingly enough, however, when the Russians sang an English folk song in English, the audience response was electric - deep silence during the song, and then deafening, continuous applause. The audience felt completely at one with the singers."

On Union rights he writes;

"A large and important category of folk and related songs springs from the ranks of workers, farmers and others active in the struggle for a better life here on earth now and in the future...

Working class and peace songs are international by nature and know no barriers. They are cultural tools which have sharp political edges to cut through racism, hypocrisy, lies and slander.

103

They can help to open our eyes to the horizon that was beheld by the great pioneers of the working class movement, who first saw the gleam of a better future. Songs inspire and encourage us to take action to realise that dream, the dream of socialism, peace and international solidarity.

Militant Negro spirituals, and protest songs, trade union and peace movement songs are used more directly than other songs as weapons by the progressive movement. Their message is forceful and clear and lays bare the class antagonisms. All these songs are used in the fight to win and maintain trade union rights, improve the standard of living, win equal rights for all citizens and oppose the war policies of the British and American governments."

On racism he writes;

"Racialism has become a serious factor in British life...

In pre-war Britain it was the British citizens of Jewish faith who were the scapegoat to the British fascists. The fascists claimed that millions of Jews were ruining the country. Upon them was laid the blame for all the evils of the capitalist system...

Today there are in Britain about 1,000,000 Commonwealth citizens. The fact that they are not white makes them easy victims for abuse. Upon this minority the present day racialists make their attack ...It is these people who are today blamed for the housing shortage and other problems which have long beset the capitalist system...

The fight against racialism and fascism is waged by the progressive movement in Britain. This includes the Communist Party, progressive people in the Labour Party, students' organisations, the trade union movement and others who ally themselves with progressive causes."

He continues on the theme of music at work;

"The practical value still today of music and song while working has not been overlooked in modern industry. Although it is usually impossible to hear an ordinary human voice speaking, let alone singing, above the noise of the machinery, the problem has been solved to some extent by relaying songs and music at enormous volumes over loudspeakers."

He discusses sea shanties in particular saying;

"Sea shanties were the work songs of the sailors in the days of the sailing vessels...

Beginning with the late 18th century, an enormous expansion of world trade had taken place ... The crews were men assembled, often impressed or shanghaied, from every nationality in the world and spoke different languages. English was the common language in which work orders were given and signals were called... The only means of getting the job done efficiently was to coordinate the efforts of a gang of sailors precisely and thus get the maximum effect at the same moment. This was the reason for the existence of the shanties. The shantyman called the signals for the work in his verses, while the crew responded pulling or pushing during the refrain...

The era of the sea shanty is a lesson in the way of life of the hard, tough men who manned the sailing vessels and battled their way across the oceans. It is a story of hardships, incredibly bad working conditions, courage, and rebellions ruthlessly put down..."

He notes other differing purposes of folk songs such as cowboy songs and writes;

"The memory of many popular heroes connected with various historical causes and events has been kept fresh in mind through the medium of folk songs...

Love, more often than not unhappy love, has been the subject of folk songs for centuries...

Folk songs are particularly helpful in teaching oral aspects of phonetics, intonation, rhythm and expression, as well as vocabulary and grammar...

Folksongs are not only a source of language acquisition and aesthetic experience, they also help to increase our factual knowledge of other countries...

Finally, folk songs serve as a cultural weapon. Like a two-way mirror, they show on the one side the reflection of our own history in the inspiring struggle of the ordinary people in other lands, striving to attain a better life and make the world a better place in which to live. The other side reveals the long perspective of historical, geographical, economic and social development of these other nations.

Overcoming the barriers of time and space through the medium of folk song, we share the past, the present, and the visions of the future of the vast majority of the people whose language we are learning and we recognise that their sorrows, their laughter, their defeats and their triumphs are our own."

Cyril released a record in 1971 entitled "British and American Songs" which he also had published through Verlag Enzyklopedia in Leipzig, East Germany in 1974. The excerpts of the 44 songs across 4 records take 26 minutes in total to play and feature Cyril singing the solos in a rich baritone voice. He was also the Director of Music. He sang the songs with the Student Chorus of the English Language Department Friedrich-Schiller University, Jena.

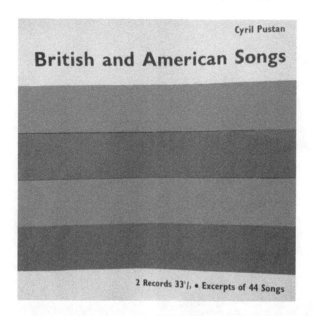

In the 1974 book of the same name, he wrote that;

"The ninety-three songs in this book are but a few bars of a great symphony - the symphony of the people who work for their daily bread and constantly strive for a better life. They are the people who in their work and play create music, the music of the people."

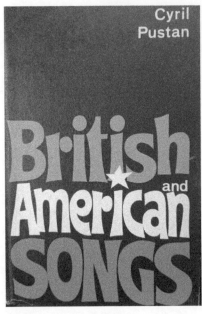
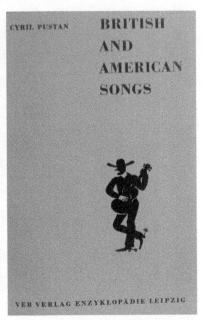

Cover   Inside frontsheet

Inscription on the gift of his book to Lieselotte Goring,
the conductor of the choir on the record

Cyril also wrote stories including *"London's Burning"*. *"Pickles"* is a story about the problems a pickling factory had in London in 1943 and may be a story written from first-hand knowledge. *"A Little story to keep you warm"* is Baa Baa Black Sheep from the sheep's point of view (3 October 1970). *"Hickory, dickory, dock..."* is an autobiography of a clock.

"An Act of Fidelity" is a story he wrote while in London, probably in 1962 as he was still at Hemsworth Court, about a walking holiday in Belgium by 2 men, one of whom he called Harry. This was at the same time as the San Francisco to Moscow March for Peace Western Europe section, as the men discuss this, where one of them has an affair with a girl called Pirkha and a fight with her husband ensues.

He used a similar theme in *"Walk for Health"* where 2 men, Harry and Cyril, go on a walking holiday initially through France, Belgium and Germany. They get the ferry from Southampton to Le Havre and are arrested on entering France as it was thought they were demonstrating about health service provision. After they were refused entry, they went to Ostend in Belgium where Pirkha also appears. Johan, the husband of her friend Astrid who Harry had an affair with has a fight with Cyril over a suggestion that it was Cyril who had the affair. One of the girls on the 1961 Peace March was called Astrid and one of the men was Johan.

"Fate" was a story about the theft of jewels by a butler from his employer and the death of the thief, fence, and murderer of both, and the recovery of the jewels by the owner.

Under the pseudonym Cecil Plummer he wrote *"The Pie was Enjoyed by All"* which is about an Englishman attending a language course in Erfurt, a town near Jena in July 1964. It is autobiographical. Pie refers to the Pedagogical Institute of Erfurt.

Cyril taught teachers of German from England, France, Finland, Norway, the Netherlands, Belgium, Cuba, California, and India.

His room was on the fifth floor and was roomy and light. Food was a buffet. Some studied the language, some the literature, and some the educational system and visited various educational institutions. A cooperative farm was visited. They visited Buchenwald. Some stayed on after the course and visited Dresden, Leipzig, and Jena.

In addition to writing books, and singing on and producing a record, he wrote poetry such as *"English Teachers' Song during Strike"* and *"Unplayed Sonatine for Trumpet and Piano"* which is a poem about a concert in Jena. He taught a poetry class in Berlin.

Despite his lack of faith, he never forgot his Jewish roots, and in one of his song sheets alongside the music and lyrics, he included the title in Hebrew.

Victor knew Cyril was Jewish but does not recall Cyril mentioning it.

All this having been to school from the age of 5 to 10, being in school for 6 months when he was 13, and having left school before his 14th birthday.

His view of the education system

In his lecture in about 1965 he wrote;

"If you are willing to accept a dead end job, a job with no prospects no future and no training these can be found. To most employers young labour is cheap labour, to be employed as long as it is remains cheap and then to be dismissed when the worker is old enough to ask for a better wage.

I am speaking specifically of the type of person who has had what is today termed a secondary modern education where there are 30 40 or more in a class where the streaming has taken the best off to other schools. Where the average teacher is at his or her wits end to keep the class quiet and disciplined, to collect the milk money and do the various duties that teachers have to do, and which themselves have nothing to do with teaching. In many cases teaching is subsidiary and it is only the new enthusiast, or the dedicated individual who tries to give the children something that will benefit them in their lives.

For the fortunate pupil who has gone to a grammar school, or has had the advantage of a progressive comprehensive school and has managed to attain a level of academic achievement with some passes in the ordinary or advanced level of the general certificate of education, the situation is somewhat different. They may be lucky enough of course to get entrance to university. There are openings in banks, offices, insurance companies, managerial positions, or the civil service. These jobs are fairly well paid, there is security of employment insofar as one can have security in a capitalist society. The jobs carry a superannuation, subsidised lunches are given in the form of luncheon vouchers. There are holidays with pay and so on..."

He goes on to talk about his view of young people at work;

"The white collar jobs tend to create an elite type of worker, indeed someone who no longer considers himself a worker but to the social grouping above. This may be particularly true of the civil service. These workers despite their grievances are far better off than any industrial worker. They have guaranteed employment, generous sick leave with pay, and many other conditions denied to most other workers. Many of them are not satisfied with this and want more, good luck to them. However the young worker in the civil service from the age of 16 or whenever he joins up till the age of 25 is considered a junior and does not receive top pay in his scale until he reaches the age of 25. For instance in the field of telegraphy or telephones a young fully trained boy or girl of 16 or 17 will be sitting among men and women doing exactly the same work. Maybe the youngster is more eager and industrious and is doing more work than his elders but it makes no difference. They must wait until they are 25 before they reach equality. Many private firms pirate these youngsters away from the civil service by offering them more money. But the government departments are basically so reactionary and hidebound that they fail to see that the youth are the future of an industry and it is the youth who should be encouraged.

The problems of young workers irrespective of their employment have many similarities. Making friends, mixing with people, earning a living, domestic problems, finding their feet in life, getting engaged, getting married, settling down, or the problem of finding somewhere to live at a reasonable rental, conflicts with parents and in-laws, the problems of bringing up a family, the everyday problems of day to day struggle to make ends meet, and of course the problem of the unsettled situation in the political arena. These problems are faced both by the so called white collar workers and the industrial workers."

He then focuses on the problems facing young industrial workers;

"Lads and lasses are turned loose at the tender age of 15 to shift for themselves in an unsympathetic world. There are of course many dead end jobs, although in some parts of Britain there are young people who have left school one, two or three years ago and have not yet found a job, and have been unemployed from the day they left school. The young worker can go into a clothing factory and work as a machinist. He can work on a building site as a labourer, get a job as a messenger boy, or a junior salesman. But the opportunities to learn a really skilled job are rare. Certain trades can be learnt through the apprenticeship scheme. This means that the young worker agrees to work until the age of 21 at low grades of pay and is indeed again a source of cheap labour. What he learns during his period of apprenticeship depends upon the type of craftsmen he works with. If they are good craftsmen all is well, if not all is not well. There is an agreement in the building industry that all apprentices must attend a trade school one day a week during their apprenticeship and they should also be attending evening classes at least two or three evenings a week. A few apprentices decline to attend classes because theory is not for them. In the technical school they have many good instructors. They also have not so good instructors. It is largely a matter of luck what type of mate you get at work and what type of instructor you get at the technical college. One has to remember too that techniques are continually advancing and unless the instructor keeps abreast of advancements, he is isolated in his college workshop or classroom and becomes out of touch.

The apprenticeship system is one form of training. Another method is to become a mate, that is an assistant, to a carpenter, or a plumber, or an electrician, or a painter, or a plasterer, or a slater and tiler, or a roofing asphalter and hope thereby to learn from these people. This again depends upon the type of person with whom you work and their willingness to teach you - many of these men do not want to teach you. There are cases on record where the mate has to stand 3 feet away from the craftsman. When the craftsman wants a hammer, he calls out boy hammer, or a wood plane, and the boy would bring a plane. And when the tool has been handed to him you stand back three feet again and await your next order. If of course something is heavy and has to be lifted or needs holding in position then of course you can hold it, but if a particularly intricate job is being done and you are not wanted to learn the trade secrets, then you are sent for an errand so that you don't see how the thing is done. Many of these men are old, cantankerous, bad tempered, or just petty and spiteful...

Yet another method to learn a trade is to go to evening classes in the appropriate subject and take a course which leads eventually to qualifying examinations. There are some drawbacks to this. The shortage of classes is one of these. In the whole of the inner London area there are only four institutes which teach bricklaying and assuming at the most taking into consideration the workshop facilities, we can assume that there is an average intake of about eighty students a year. This applies to most of the other trades too so in this field and through this method the annual training programme is very small.

Young workers are mostly unorganised and membership to craft trade unions is not always easy to obtain. There is a hangover to the old days when unions affected by the anti-competition laws were practically secret societies and had a swearing in ceremony...

I introduced many young fellows to the union that I met on the jobs and actually I did so even when I knew them not to be good craftsman, and I always made this clear at lodge meetings. Because it was better the union had some control over them than they were unorganised.

There is another side to attending evening classes in order to do so. It means you have to leave work at least by five pm. in order to get home, washed and changed because most jobs have no washing facilities, nor water, at most you wash your hands out of a dirty bucket. So under such circumstances you don't come to work in decent clothes. This means you have to go home and change. Often too the job of employment is a long way from home. I am speaking of London which is a big place. You might on occasions have to leave work an hour or two before time and lose the wages for this time. Not only that, many peoples wages especially the wage of young workers are supplemented by overtime earnings.

It is a fact some years ago and probably still is that although the official working week is shorter the actual hours worked are longer. It is not uncommon to see a job advertised in the newspapers or trade journals in which one of the attractive features is plenty of overtime. And many young people will not consider a job with under 50 hours a week, because only by working long hours can they get a decent living wage to enable them to buy the latest type of suit, run their motorbike or scooter or even car if they are the ambitious type. The young worker is easy prey for the ad men.

The styles are always changing. The most fantastic clothes are sold at fantastic prices. For many the allure of bowling alleys, pin tables, dance halls, the television, and public houses are far stronger than attending evening classes. As it is, the generally more serious minded go, and for all that the classes are overcrowded.

There is little incentive to go to classes. A person who spent four, five, six or sometimes more years at classes having given up weekends and evenings, will earn no more than someone who is totally illiterate. Actually if he is careful with his work and does it as it should be done he may even learn less because on bonus work you are paid by output independently of quality.

Many of the supervisory jobs go to men who are not qualified but have driving power, that is power to drive the men to work harder, and often the younger worker is the easier to exploit while they are not aware of the methods of the bosses and consider something clever to work hard against themselves or the clock. An employer once said to me we don't need qualified men or even good tradesman for supervisory jobs, we need someone who can organise and keep the job running smoothly, in other words someone who can make the others work."

6

Later years

Time in England while living in East Germany

After he went to East Germany, despite the salary which while relatively good in East German terms was meagre as far as the United Kingdom was concerned, he sent money every month to his parents and wrote regularly. He visited 3 or 4 times a year and stayed with them when in London for weeks at a time. He took numerous pictures of Ella's children with the Box Brownie camera he took out of his large camera cases that were packed with lenses, tripods, light meters, and all sorts of gadgets a professional would be proud of. He sometimes took cine films. As the family photographer, he was rarely in the pictures. He took his equipment with him whenever he went out. He took Sally and Jeffrey on some outings, but rarely Michael and Stanley (Sally's brothers). Sally remembers him riding a motorbike and using the bus. Jeffrey remembers a yellow camper van. He had a full driving license valid from 27 January 1976. When they asked what his job was, he would say he was a road sweeper or dustbin man.

Michael, Max, Regina
Ella, Pepe (family friend), Esther, Sally
Stanley, Jeffrey, Susan the dog
Taken in about 1971 by Cyril

Cyril's with his camera bag   His favourite Box Brownie

While visiting, he did a short Post Graduate course in Closed Circuit Television in Education at the University of London Goldsmith College in the Spring term of 1971. He studied for a Post Graduate Diploma in Phonetics at Leeds University in the 1971 to 1972 semester, noted the bus transport problems in an article in "Pulse" on 25 March 1972, and sought to expand his education and employment prospects.

20 Ralph Mount,
Leeds, 6
Yorks.

8.4.1971

The Director
Huddersfield College of Education (Technical)

Dear Sir,

I have seen the pamphlet "Teaching in Technical Colleges" and would appreciate having the opportunity to find out at first-hand about the full-time plumbing teacher training course run at your college, and employment prospects after having taken such a course.

I am 43 years of age and at present am taking a Postgraduate course at Leeds University.

I am free to come at any time until the commencement of the new term (April 20th). After that date I could attend on the afternoon of any Wednesday or Thursday or at any time on Fridays.

Yours faithfully,

His lesson plan on 20 October 1972 explained that its aim was; *"to give during conversation periods a working class background of historical events that play such a large part in political life in Britain today.*

By this one does not give a history lesson but one draws lessons from history during discussion and attempts to show how these things tie up. For example: the Chartist movement in the 1830s; revolt on the Clyde and unrest during the first world war; struggles of the unemployed in the inter-war years; the fight against fascism; student unrest; the work-in on the Clyde. Although separated in time these events are linked together in history, and they show that the British working class may be slow at times but they will not allow anybody to walkover them for too long.

I have attempted to show how the trade union movement and political parties conduct meetings, organise a congress, discuss resolutions. Without this basic knowledge it is not possible to understand the political system in Britain...

To be able to talk to people and value them as human beings, one must know people, their background, the idiosyncrasies. Above all, one must learn to respect other people. These are a few of the things I try to do not only with the groups we are discussing but with every group I teach."

It was during this period that Cyril's stepson, Bobby Fischer was headline news throughout the world due to playing and beating Boris Spassky in the World Chess Championship in Iceland in 1972. Regina visited during the series of games to Bobby's consternation according to Brad Darrach. Cyril met Regina's daughter Joan and her son Nicholas on two separate trips when Nicholas was 8 and 6. Nicholas remembered Cyril as being *"an extremely strong and muscular man, with a wonderful sense of humour and always full of song – some labor folk song "I dreamed I saw Joe Hill last night" others of them ribald. "My father was the keeper of London Zoo"*. Nicholas remembers that

"Regina and he had a deep affection, and that she was always happier when she was with him. His intellect, humour and warmth made a lasting impression."

While in England he travelled widely and wrote to friends about the characters he met at boarding houses.

He wrote to a friend, George on 27 June 1973, *"most lawyers are crooks – especially when they smell pickings and the few that are honest are generally not too competent."* Lutz Hummel, recollects that Cyril, like many East German's believed that *"lawyers were paragraph acrobats"* given their political appointment and lack of independence. Cyril loved photography and wrote to a friend, Stewart on 6 June 1973, about many of its technicalities. Lutz remembered his love of photography and use of the University photography facilities.

The United Kingdom Cyril visited in the 1970s was very different to the one he had left in 1962. The Conservative Party under Edward Heath was back in power after nearly 6 years of Labour government. His attempt to reform the Unions led to strikes, a 3-day week, power cuts, and defeat in the 1974 election to Labour. Cyril would have inevitably supported the Unions. It is not clear what Cyril would have thought about the United Kingdom joining the European Economic Area, as, despite it leading to greater international co-operation and less chance of war between Western European countries, it created a Capitalist power block on the doorstep of the Warsaw Pact.

Relationship with Regina

They wrote many letters and postcards to each other when they were not together, such as when Cyril was in London in June 1967 going to various universities and when he sent a postcard every day, or often caused by Regina attending conferences or doing short term jobs elsewhere such as Autumn 1974 when she was in London. On one occasion when Regina's grandson Alexander was with her in London, Cyril and Alexander visited Ella and Max at the factory where they worked and had tea.

Of her feelings for Cyril, Regina told the New York Times in an interview on 17 October 1972 while campaigning for Senator George McGovern in the US Presidential election that "*It was sort of like robbing the cradle...but he made me an offer I couldn't refuse.*"

Cyril wrote to Regina on 17 November 1972 saying;

"To work effectively man must use his intelligence. The human frame alone, powerful as it is as an organism, is yet relatively uneconomical as a sole unit of power and work. One must use as levers for effectiveness mediums that appeal to the intellect. One should get more out of an effort than one puts into it. Jail may get publicity, but if one's actions are not in keeping with general public feelings, then instead of support one gets insults, blame, and kicks from all sides.

There are many ways of doing things and of not doing things. One must appeal to reason, not to emotions – which may not coincide with yours. Mental violence, and aggressiveness alienate, while reason attracts reasonable people and convinces them...

I respect and admire you as a person. I admire your integrity, your abilities, your humaneness, your kindness..."

Esther used to fret whenever Regina visited that she would be arrested for some reason or other, as visits invariably coincided with demonstrations or rallies, and she was often seen on television demonstrating. Esther would hold her head in her hands. She was convinced that the telephone was bugged due to Regina's activism.

Ella said that Regina lay down in the roads to stop the traffic in an attempt to stop the closure of a Women's hospital, and described her as an amazing woman who had had a very hard life. Regina wanted to change the world. She left a van outside Ella's house she had used to travel the world. This may be the yellow van Jeffrey remembered.

Victor remembers that Regina and Cyril were often apart as Regina was away a lot in places such as Nicaragua, and the United States. Sally remembers that Cyril and Regina often visited London without each other. After 1971, Regina had various short term locum jobs in Plymouth, Derby, Leeds, Exeter, Belfast and various hospitals in and around London generally in Paediatrics.

Problems later in life

Cyril told Ella that Regina struggled to find work in East Germany where there was no shortage of doctors, and she thought of leaving Jena to make a difference abroad.

Among Cyril's papers were a large collection of mint East German stamps which were gifts from his neighbour Christine to Ella. He had given Christine 2 sets of British stamps on the BBC and Famous Men.

Cyril's work ethic was summarised in a letter he wrote on 17 September 1974 to Lieselotte Goring who had been the conductor of the choir on the record, *"Hasty, slap-dash work, irrespective of results and merely for effect is not my way of working…"*

His mood had changed as he wrote to Lieselotte, *"I am so rarely, these days, in a mood for singing…"*

He never blamed others as he wrote *"Your performance yesterday was not bad. Because we had no chance to practice together beforehand it was I who was completely off key during the whole situation. Also, dear Liselotte, even should you make a mistake while accompanying, please do not apologise, etc. Please put the mistake down to me."*

Cyril was also a model for the works of others

Victor remembers vague rumours that Cyril and Regina did not get on, lived largely separate lives, and had separated. He thought that Cyril may have become involved with a younger woman.

On 23 May 1975 Regina divorced Cyril in Jena. It is not clear what the reason for the divorce was. They still shared the Jena apartment, saw each other, and corresponded. Cyril's family were unaware of the divorce. He was a proud man and telling them would inevitably have led to the response from Chaim *"I told you so."*

Cyril wrote to Regina on 30 November 1975;

"You don't have to live in a "twilight" world or a world of "uncertainty". I have told you this a dozen times; nor have you anything to be jealous about. And I can assure you that your 'taking off' won't in any way make me happy or improve my situation. I don't want you to leave and I have no intention of helping you to leave; and facts are beside the added factor that you should also consider that you can't run around like a nineteen year old any more..."

And on 14 December 1975;

"You need to be centred in one place and have some stability and security. I have said it before; you (and I) are not nineteen year

old chicks. It's time to think of settling down. Here, you have some stability, and financial security. I know these things don't worry you, but they are worth considering. Also, you are not on your own."

On holiday

In late January 1976, despite being divorced, Cyril and Regina went on holiday to Portugal for a week and wrote a pamphlet about their experience.

They wrote;

"...late in January 1976 we decided to take our week's holiday in Portugal, away from the freezing sleety winter and the influenza

epidemic in Britain. Friends had warned us not to risk our lives by foolishly taking a trip to a country where they imagined shootings, bombings and arson were the order of the day. They were forgetting what goes on daily in Britain, Northern Ireland and America. We went to Portugal on our own, not knowing anyone there, and were able to see for ourselves something of what is really happening in Portugal.

By now we have almost forgotten the record breaking downpours of rain we met and the influenza, which proved inescapable after all...

We had been riding around in Lisbon ...on top of a double decker bus. From it we spotted a large white banner of the Women's Democratic Movement... The sign was stretched across the entire top floor of an old building ...When we went in we noticed a poster saying that a trip was leaving for a cooperative farm. We had paid up at once..."

They had shared a room and got up at 4:30 to make it in time for the bus which was due to leave at 6. It actually left at 7.40. They wrote;

"A pleasant faced woman was sitting in front of us...She pointed out our destination. It was across the width of Portugal, only a few miles from the Spanish border. We had a trip of 200 kilometres (125 miles ahead of us)...Soon after we got out on the highway people started coming up to the microphone at the front of the bus. Some recited or sang solo. Some led the others in singing popular songs of the revolution or folk songs...

As soon as we arrived at the farm, it was announced that lunch was ready. We were pleasantly surprised. We had been told to bring food for two days and had done so, but were not particularly looking forward to two days of sandwiches and bottled drinks...

After lunch everyone climbed into open trucks pulled by tractors and we went out to pick olives. The ground was wet and muddy. We could feel the soles of our shoes being pulled downwards at every step...

In the evening the tractors came to pick us up and take us back to the farmyard for supper...

We all lined up at the various cooking pots and took or were ladled out what we wanted. By this time it was too dark to see what you were eating. But whatever it was it tasted very good. There was no electricity. The only light came from oil lamps in the shed and the cooking fires in the courtyard...

One of the organisers asked whether we had brought any blankets along. We had none. ...We heard we were to sleep in a palace... For many years ...the palaces had been standing empty and unused. Absentee ownership was the rule. The landlords generally lived in Lisbon or abroad...

It had been a long day and we were about ready to fall asleep on our feet. But another of the organisers told us the sleeping arrangements would be known in about half an hour. Meanwhile we could go and have a cup of coffee in a local cafe.

The cafe was packed full. With the noise of conversation, the clatter of glasses, and the constant coming and going, it was impossible to hear a sound from the television set perched on a shelf above the bar...

At least 30 women had lined up for the one toilet at the back of the cafe, the line stretching out to the front of the cafe. The line moved very slowly because the toilet had no flush system. Each person had to pour water in from a large pitcher. This had to be refilled from a faucet on one side of the walls at the side of the hall...

The women were told they could sleep in the palace...The men were to sleep in their seats on the bus...

Meantime, a film was to be shown shortly at the local cinema, we were told, and we could come and see it if we liked. Once more off the bus and a short walk to the movie, a ramshackle barnlike old building. About 500 or more local people were present waiting for the film to begin. Every seat was taken.

We climbed up to the projection room. It had no seats. You could sit on the wooden floor or stand up. If you stood you could see only the upper half of the screen. If you sat you could see the lower half. So we kept bobbing up and down. The film turned out to be a documentary about the war in North Vietnam...

It was past 11 p.m. A speaker now came out onto the movie stage and a meeting began...

The meeting was still continuing to a full house when we left the place at 1 a.m. We were very tired and decided that if we were to get any sleep it would have to be in our seats in the bus. Otherwise we would not be able to do a stroke of work the next day.

We heard snoring in the bus. Others had also decided it was time to get some sleep. We sat getting colder and colder, dozing on and off until we were aroused by tugging on our coats. "Someone has come to take you to your beds for tonight."

We were taken by a young girl to her house. It was a short distance from the square where the bus was parked for the night... It was past 3 in the morning when we got to bed...

After a breakfast of coffee and rolls, the family went with us to the town square, where tractors and trucks were waiting to pick everybody up. There was much singing of folk and revolutionary songs. Several of the young fellows from the cooperatives had really good voices. We could have listened to them all day...

We then heard over a loudspeaker that there would be no work this day. The farmers considered the ground too wet and muddy for us. Instead they decided to show us the progress being made under the agrarian reform.

We climbed into the waiting line of trucks. With red flags fluttering, the convoy started through the countryside, headed by the truck carrying the singers and guitar players...

The convoy returned to" the *"farm for lunch. Again, the women had worked hard. The cooperative had outdone itself this time, providing a tangerine apiece for everyone as dessert. After lunch the crowd had a good time dancing and singing. Then a meeting was held in the open courtyard, with the speakers up on a truck. Some told about their experiences on the farm before the revolution. Others spoke about the trials and tribulations of the cooperative. Others stressed the need for continued contact between town and country workers...*

While the meeting was going on, people from the buses were going round in the crowd selling all sorts of political pins, pamphlets and stickers put out by women's groups, trade unions, the cooperative movement and a wide spectrum of left wing organisations many of these disagreeing with each other...

About 8 p.m. the buses started for Lisbon...An old man, one of the farm workers from the cooperative, had come with us on the bus. He had had plenty of wine and was in a mellow sentimental mood. He began singing nostalgic songs and kissing everyone on the bus, the men on one cheek and the women on both. Several times he had said goodbye and got as far as the bus door. Then he came back and repeated the whole performance all over again...

We were amazed at the kindness and tolerance the people on the bus showed...and wondered whether Britons or Americans would be as good natured."

Apart from detailing what they did, they discussed the political history of Portugal, the economic situation, medical care, literacy, land ownership, and the working lives of those they spent time with. They provide a vivid account of daily life amongst the working class in Portugal in and amongst their sightseeing on what many would see as an unusual holiday trip by a couple who had recently divorced.

Ill health

In 1976 he was ill with flu. He also had a prostatectomy which is a treatment for prostate cancer, and in the spring was treated for 3 weeks at St Leonard's Hospital London where he was very complimentary towards all the nursing team for the *"kindness, understanding, attention, and selfless devotion they displayed day and night to the patients in their care"* and the physiotherapist and ward orderlies *"who with clocklike regularity dutifully filled the cups that revived the thirsting souls."* Cancer UK research shows that in the 1970's the survival rate for those with prostate cancer was only 25%, but for those under the age of 50, only 2 men in 1,000,000 died of prostate cancer.

Cyril added;

"How different the world would be if people would only show the same tolerance and kindness in their everyday dealings with their fellow men..."

He spent 8 months on sick leave living in London in 1976, and only returned to Jena at the end of the year. After his return to London due to continued ill health, Regina continued with her activism and was arrested on 20 February 1977 when she camped outside the Home Office when campaigning against the deportation of 2 men who faced charges of unauthorised receipt of secret information.

He had a further admission to hospital and had written to the Friedrich-Schiller University explaining he was off work due to ill-health.

His excellent work record over many years was noted as was his ill-health in his last appraisal on 3 May 1977 where it was noted that, *"he has been absent from teaching for 9 months in the past two years due to serious illness. An increase request will not be made this year"* in relation to his salary.

Cyril never expressed regrets to Victor about moving to East Germany, but he was disturbed *"by the growing pressures of commercialism from the west and the inability of the GDR leaders to adequately confront them or find ways to overcome obvious difficulties and achieve rapport with growing sectors of the population, torn more and more by an increasing polarisation at the geographic dividing line, in Germany and Berlin, between two systems"*. Victor's overriding impression of Cyril is that he was a fine man.

7

Secrets and lies

Cyril spent much of the final 18 months of his life in London due to his ill health and the operations, and often said he did not want to return to Jena. Despite this, he felt the pull to return and the family could not persuade him to stay.

It was in September 1977 that Regina rang Ella. Ella told Samantha that Regina had said that Cyril said he felt tired, sat down, and died of a heart attack. He died on 8 September at 8pm.

He had been healthy, he did not smoke, would only drink out of his own cup or a jam jar, and he was a vegan.

Cyril was buried in the cemetery at Erb Platz Ullrich Mauer, Sud-Friedhof, Weimar which is about 12 miles from Jena on 20 September 1977. Christine said *"the grave is in a fine old churchyard, by a stone wall covered with ivy. It is a quiet place far away from the noise of the town, with high trees nearby."* His headstone was organised by Regina using the Hebrew inscription provided by Ella and Hilda and including the Star of David. She also gave Ella and Hilda the time and date of death to enable his Yahrzeit (annual memorial) to be on the correct Hebrew date of 26 Ellul.

 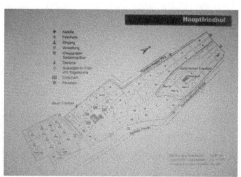

His plot is marked on the left

Christine wrote on 20 March 1979 that, *"Cyril was a very fine person, in fact he was too good, too kind and too gentle for this world. God must have known his heart and called him to himself".* Regina wrote on 1 January 1980 that, *"Cyril was very quiet... but made a lot of friends in Jena that thought very highly of him."* Christine sent Ella Cyril's papers saying on 28 November 2000 *"I am arranging all this in the memory of Cyril and Regina. They were very good friends to me. I owe them so much – I remember them with love and gratitude."*

Christine wrote on 27 April 1981 that Cyril, *"was always willing to help and to give and was himself such a modest person."*

Ella and Hilda's lie

Ella and Hilda decided not to tell Esther and Chaim that their beloved son had died as Esther was unwell having just had an operation and as she had also lost a brother. Ella had gone to tell her of the death but could not get the words out. When she left, she was crying in the street. Regina had told her initially not to tell Esther. Chaim died in 1984 and Esther in 1990 never knowing what had happened to Cyril. But they knew something was wrong as the monthly remittances, letters, and visits from this kind,

133

loving, family man, suddenly stopped. Ella said that Hilda sought advice from a Rabbi who advised her she did not need to tell Esther as he was her first born and a month had passed since the death.

They never had the heart to tell them. Cyril was not included in Esther's will.

Ella said that after his death, Hilda had Esther's post redirected to Ella as they became aware that Regina's brother Max had sent a letter of condolence. Chaim thought she had taken the remittances Cyril had sent, which of course she had not. Ella still did not tell Esther of his death. The acrimony was the last thing Cyril would have wanted, and it was caused by a secret whose origin was well intentioned but perhaps became harder to justify as time went by. Ella thought that Esther thought that Cyril had "gone off with a younger woman".

Cyril's death brought together Ella in London, Christine and Regina in Germany, and Regina's daughter Joan in America despite the vast distances between them and the lack of a common link other than Cyril. There were many letters passing between Ella, Regina, and Christine, some of them via Joan. They were all loving and caring. On 8 October 1977 Regina wrote renouncing any financial interest in Cyril's estate in favour of Esther and Chaim and in particular in relation to their property.

What is clear from reading the letters, is that all concerned only had Esther and Chaim's welfare at heart, even though others may have taken a different view as to how that was best met. None acted with malice. All suffered great pain. And all loved Cyril, Esther, and Chaim. And whilst Cyril had 7 siblings, it was only Ella and Hilda who were involved in the decisions. Sidney had chosen a path outside the Jewish community, moved to Southampton and then Ireland, and lost contact with the family. Stuart had personal issues that prevented him participating meaningfully in discussions. Frederick had died as an infant. Ivan had schizophrenia and was in residential care for most of his adult life. And Rosalie had chosen a path outside the Jewish community which reduced her contact with the family. It was because of the loses already suffered by Esther and Chaim that Ella and Hilda took the decision they did when balancing how to minimise the heart ache and suffering of their parents as best as they could.

Joan wrote on 30 November 1977 "*I am terribly sorry for all the sorrow and difficulties your family is suffering at this time*" enclosed money on Regina's behalf, and offered to find accommodation if one of the boys, probably Michael being the only one really old enough to travel abroad at that time, came to visit.

Regina wrote to Ella on 18 March 1978 saying;

"*I got a call from Bobby on Thursday this week, he asked when I was going to be in the States, and I told him I think your mother is going to ask what happened any day now and may want to come here with you ...I am still all broken up and guess I'll never get over it. But on top of that I am worried thinking your mother may be thinking it over to herself and just be afraid to ask you, if that is the case it must be very bad for her to be in that situation. And it can't go on much longer.*"

And on 13 April 1978 saying;

"*I have been wanting to phone you to ask if your mother had asked again about Cyril. I feel very bad about it and am worried she may be worrying and afraid to ask. It would really be best if you both or whoever else can come for at least a weekend and get it over with. I can't see it continuing.*"

And on 7 May 1978 saying;

"*After our phone talk yesterday I thought again of what to do. You say you still don't want to tell your mother and feel it is best not to tell her. You may be right. But I am afraid she already must feel something terrible has happened and is only afraid to ask. She'll probably do so sooner or later, if only to get rid of the uncertainty. If she phones or writes of Cyril asking why he never phones I won't be able to give her an answer, and that alone will be answer enough...I would be willing to come to England to see her and tell her myself if you agree that I should."*

And on 22 June 1978 asking *"if you want me to come there to tell your mother."*

Christine wrote to Ella on 1 October 1978 saying;

"You will, perhaps, be surprised to get a letter from Jena. I am Christine Patzer. I work at the Foreign Language Department of the University as a teacher of English. Your brother, Cyril Pustan, and I were colleagues for about 13 years. We were not only colleagues, but very good friends. His untimely death has been a severe blow to all who knew him. He was a kind and patient teacher and a true and honest person in every respect. You won't find anybody like him again. We all miss him very much. I find I can't resign myself with his death, and yet I know he has left us never to return. But I often think of him and remember the conversations we had.

The reason why I am writing to you is Cyril's mother. I suppose she must be waiting from week to week to hear from her eldest son. I am sure she must suffer a lot not knowing the reason for his silence. He used to phone her regularly, at least once a month. Now she has hasn't received a letter, or a post-card, or a call for more than a year. For how long can the sad truth be hidden from her and his father? I am worried she might phone or write here one day...the thought that she might phone me one day, and ask me about Cyril depresses me very much. I wouldn't know what to say, I feel I could never tell her the truth, nor could I give her an evasive answer."

The response from Hilda on 10 October 1978 was;

"My sister and I appreciate your kind sentiment and feelings but wish you to know the following. We both feel most strongly that we do not want our mother to know about Cyril and we are convinced that such an action would lead to the entirely death of our mother, something Cyril would not have wished. We can see no benefit in having anguish and sorrow for the remaining years of their life. She is also frail and in poor health as is her husband. We wish you to know that it is completely and utterly against our wishes that our mother should be informed of his passing."

Chaim wrote to Cyril and Regina on 26 November 1978 saying *"I have written to you and received no reply. Mum and I are terribly worried"*. Esther wished Bobby all the best in his forthcoming chess match.

Regina wrote to Ella on 13 December 1978 saying;

"I haven't got the nerve to write to your mother directly...I live in dread of a phone call from her to Mrs Patzer or to Joanie. Mrs P doesn't know what she would say and she is a terrible liar, she would never succeed in carrying it off at all, it is just not in her. Joanie positively will not tell any lies and your mother will know something happened." Indeed, Regina had written to Ella and Hilda on 8 October 1977 saying that Bobby would not lie about seeing him when he had not.

She wrote to Ella on 2 January 1979 saying;

"I think your mother will notice there is never anything from Cyril or by him. It just is a hopeless effort from the start. But if you are decided not to say anything to her, I won't go against it...I really feel your mother may be suffering more not knowing that if she is told. But I would not go against your wishes. I feel sure you have gone through a terrible time and are still doing so."

Having returned to the USA Regina wrote to Ella on 14 November 1979 saying, *"I worry and think about your mother all the time.*

137

She surely must worry and wonder herself. How has she been all this time?"

The deception played on Christine's mind very much and she wrote to Ella on 14 January 1980 *"My thoughts are very often with Regina, with you and with Cyril's parents. May the Lord have mercy upon us."*

Esther and Chaim continued to write to Cyril not knowing he had died. On 26 February 1979 Esther wrote to Cyril and Regina saying, *"I thank you for your phone call to Hilda, sorry I did not hear you and Cyril myself, try and write to me more often both of you as it cheers us all up no end..."*

They sent him birthday cards, saying *"it's some time since we have seen you back"*, and telling him of Sally and Jeffrey's A level choices in March 1980. On 15 December 1980 Esther wrote *"I would very much like to hear from you, as if you are in touch with Ella she does not let me know how you are keeping. I do worry about you both."* She also sent birthday cards. These letters and cards were returned by Christine to Ella at Ella's request.

Christine wrote to Ella on 14 February 1982 saying *"I often think of your mother. I was very sad I had to put down the receiver on her the other day."*

Both Christine and Regina invited Ella to visit East Germany, but Ella always declined. She hardly ever left London and never once left England throughout her entire life. She and Max hosted Regina's brother Max and his wife Irma one evening when they were in London in late 1981.

Regina's secret

Regina had said that Cyril said he felt tired, sat down, and died of a heart attack.

He did not.

The autopsy report identified the cause of death as suicide by hanging, this also being recorded in the file held by the Stasi, the East German Secret Police.

Regina wrote to the Friedrich-Schiller University on 15 September 1977. The letter was written in English. The University insisted it be written in German. The letter says;

"I am writing to you in the hope of clarifying the possible reasons for the suicide of Cyril Pustan, language teacher at the Friedrich-Schiller University in Jena on 8 September 1977.

I think he had the overwhelming feeling that he neither wanted nor could bring himself to go back to his work, a feeling brought about by an accumulation of what he felt to be disappointments and injustices during his years as a language teacher in Jena from 1963 to 8 September 1977.

Here are just a few examples that I happen to know...

1. Educational television

A few years ago he attended a three month winter course on educational television for teaching purposes, at Goldsmith College, University of London. He had a long battle to get permission and was given the impression that he should not participate in the course and that the university in Jena was not interested in his activity in this direction, it would be his own business. He took the course at his own expense, paid the travel himself, the tuition fees and the daily living expenses. On his return he was enthusiastic about the value of educational television in teaching English and had gained hands-on experience in the field. At that time people with this kind of training were rare, and the technical facilities for in school training television were available in both Jena and Halle. He was not given the opportunity to use his education.

2. *Phonetics Course at the University of Leeds 1971*

Cyril wanted to qualify through further studies in England. He asked what subject the University of Jena considered useful, he would be willing to study whatever would be considered necessary and what he could use in English lessons on his return.

He was told that the University was not interested in any study, that he did not need any further qualifications to be able to carry out his conversation exercises which would be all they want from him. Finally, he went to the Ministry of Higher Education in Berlin and got permission to study in England.

Because of the delay in getting the permit, he arrived in England very late. The only course that was still available was a Phonetics course at the University of Leeds. He enrolled on this at his own expense and took unpaid leave from Jena. When he returned to Jena, his knowledge was not evaluated. He was told that he was not needed for phonetics lessons. He was not given recognition.

The phonetics course was extremely difficult for him because he did not have the theoretical and academic basis in that field that other students on the course began with as a prerequisite. He did not give up and worked very hard.

He continued to study phonetics with books which he bought in England, until he was assigned to teach phonetics lessons 5 or 6 years later in 1977. He prepared many teaching materials for his classes using his own initiatives and free time to make them.

In the spring of 1977 when the question of the wage increase arose, he was passed over as he would have been in England for part of the time where he was hospitalised and undergoing surgery. The small wage increase of 35 or 50 DDM a month would not affect him. But he did not like it because his tireless efforts to master the basics of phonetics to be able to teach it at University were not recognised.

3. *Regional studies as a basis for studying the English language*

A few years ago he was told he could teach this subject in seminars and lectures. He bought visual teaching aids and collected teaching materials and texts and made many colour slides for this purpose during his vacation in England. Eventually he was told that someone else would teach the subject instead. No reason was given. It seemed to him that as an Englishman he was at least in a certain degree more qualified than a foreigner. He was seriously interested in the subject and done a lot to prepare for it. He asked for permission to attend the Regional Studies conference for this, but this was not arranged.

4. *Herder Institute*

Cyril had asked several times to be allowed to attend courses at the Herder Institute in Leipzig, at least for a limited time. He wanted to be able to deal intensively in German at least for a short time in an atmosphere where everyone learned the basics of the language and everyone around him spoke German. He wanted to be in a learning situation where his teachers and curriculum were adapted to the needs of foreigners.

He had tried to take German lessons at the University of Jena, but the basics and the level of the students were very different. There was always a succession of different teachers with different methods and different materials. It was difficult to attend regularly or to do the homework assignments because of the pressure of the work, and in any case, he only had contact with Germans this way a few hours a week.

He was only spoken to in English whether by a teacher student or scientist at every opportunity. He was told he was here to speak English, did not need to know German, and that if he wanted to learn German that was his private matter. He wanted very much to be able to read the newspaper on the day it was published instead of having to wait for the Morning Star to appear. He wanted to be able to actively participate in conferences and events, to be able to converse with others, including teachers who could not speak English, and he wanted to break out of the isolation caused by a lack of basic knowledge of German. Once he had this foundation, he would have been able to continue in classes and in self-study. There were never any conversations with him or any arrangements made because of the Herder Institute.

In early 1975, Cyril had attempted suicide but was saved." The Stasi file identifies it was in February 1974 and it failed as Regina came home early. *"Professor Wietschorek from the Psychiatric Clinic found no psychiatric anomalies, but he did send the University a recommendation that Cyril should be allowed to attend the Herder Institute in order to break the vicious circle of his language isolation. Nothing was done. Cyril was not informed of this. There was no debate, neither approval nor rejection.*

At first Cyril could not believe that the matter was being completely ignored. He waited a long time for something to be told to him or for something to happen. It made it difficult for him that this problem was ignored, especially because if he learned German, it would also be useful for the university in the long run.

Almost two years later, in October 1976, a colleague began giving him one-to-one German lessons, and at that time he was beginning to make real progress.

5. <u>Accommodation</u>

Since Cyril's arrival in Jena in 1963 he lived in an attic that was originally used to dry clothes, assuming that this would only be temporary when he moved in. This made it necessary to live in a small room of only a few square metres, to cook, to study, to prepare, to stack books and magazines and to sleep in this room even in winter. The accommodation had no bath, shower, or laundry facilities, only bucket and bowls that had to be heated on the coal stove.

You could not walk around there. You could only stand upright in the centre. Clothes, books, magazines or records that were stored in one of the storage rooms on the side became mouldy and smelly because of the humidity. In winter, ice crystals glittered on the wall of the room. The other storage room was actually the toilet, which also had a sink. Clothing, food, and kitchen utensils had to be stored in it.

When he was later asked why he had not asked for housing earlier or threatened that he would leave if he did not obtain a reasonable apartment after so many years, Cyril said he did not want to take away living space from GDR families with children, if it were so scarce. He thought the University would offer him an apartment knowing his situation, if there were enough apartments available. He would not take another apartment from others who needed it.

Other employees who started their teaching after Cyril were given apartments. No other English teacher among Cyril's acquaintances had to live under Cyril's living conditions. Even in the house in which he lived Brandströmstraße 20 Cyril's room was left out and apparently it was not considered necessary to take care of it as it was only a temporary accommodation, when new sinks were installed, and other changes were made to the 3 apartments in the house.

Various families moved in and out of two apartments in the house during those years, but Cyril did not find out about this until the new family moved in. He was never offered anything. After his attempted suicide in early 1975" it was in February 1974, *"requests were made to review his living conditions.*

143

A committee of 5 people confirmed that the accommodation was unreasonable and did not meet the minimum standards. An immediate move was necessary as an urgent measure.

About 6 months later Cyril was offered an apartment in Kahla which he refused. Among other things, there would have been additional difficulties getting to work, as he often had courses in Jena early in the morning and late in the evening. In 1976 he was finally offered an apartment in Jena which his colleague had taken over for him when he was sick abroad. Upon his return he improved the apartment with his own work and money. Provisions were made to install better heating, bath and shower and he was about to move in ... when he passed away...

6. *Reporting on his work*

He felt overburdened by constantly having to submit special protocols, and reports of his time and work. They took up considerable paperwork and robbed him of time to prepare for the class which was already taking more time than he had. He found out from other English teachers at other universities in the GDR, such constant detailed protocols and reports were not required from them.

7. *Editing of translations and making tapes*

Cyril was overburdened by constantly having to revise translations that had nothing to do with his teaching duties. Practically every time, he refused to take payment in the hope he would not to be obliged to do further work, but the fact that he refused money while Intertext or others charged fees meant that more translations were given to him. They were often highly specialised scientific subjects of which he had no basic knowledge. They therefore required additional work on his part to be able to understand what he had to revise or which English expressions were used. He often worked on these texts late at night or on weekends when he needed more time to prepare his own courses or to rest. He also made corrections in publications or in speeches to be delivered at congresses abroad and made voice recordings for tapes for practising the oral presentation.

I remember that a few years ago he made 20 tape recordings with literary material for the Institute for the Blind in Leipzig without payment. In 1977 he made a series of tapes for a school in Naumburg which took about 80 hours of work. Since he was the only Englishman in the area many requests to the department were turned over to him for completion.

He asked other English teachers teaching English in the GDR if they had the same problem and found that they were not so stressed and were expected to concentrate on their work. Cyril could never refuse a request, as anyone who came to him wanting manuscripts revised assumed that was part of his job.

No official rule has ever been established or made known to centralise the whole problem and to protect him from the constant damage to his time and health.

8. *Slide show for the Friendship Society GDR/Great Britain*

In 1969 and 1970 Cyril bought cameras and films in order to produce a series of different slide shows about the GDR, one of which was about the 5th Sports Festival in Leipzig in 1969. The slides were shown to various groups in London and elsewhere in England, arranged by various progressive organisations there. Many of the slides were also used in Cyril's lectures at Jena University. This project was carried out at his own expense.

In June 1977 the Friendship Society of GDR/Great Britain in London wrote to ask the Friedrich-Schiller University to help Cyril prepare a slide show of the 6th Sports Festival and Children's Spartakiad in Leipzig from 25 to 31 July 1977. There was no reply to this letter. In response to Cyril's inquiry in Jena, he was *told that the University had not asked him to do this and therefore could not support him. It was his private matter.*

Cyril was given permission for a workers' weekly ticket at a reduced fare for the train journey between Leipzig and Jena ... He was also able to make various trips to the light meter factory in Weimar when his light meter broke and finally had to be replaced. A large part of his savings were spent on this project, for travel, food in Leipzig, repair and replacement of broken devices, films, slide frames, development etc.

He intended to go to London to show the slides on the public holidays of October 7, 8, and 9 but that would have made up 44 hours of train and boat travel for the one day in London and another 500 Marks from his own pocket - airfare is much higher.

Cyril showed letters that the project was supported by the Lecture Bureau of the London Cooperative Society and Gordon Shaffer, the Lenin Prize winner, but it seemed to Cyril that the University did not consider his efforts worthy of support. He notes bitterly that after all his efforts, these slides could probably not be shown as intended in London on the 28th anniversary of the GDR.

From time to time in the past, especially in the days leading to up to his tragic death, Cyril said he felt disappointed, a failure, overworked and exhausted. He said he was needed because of the lack of staff at the time and that he could not just be absent from work at the beginning of the semester unless he was sick, and saw no way out. He felt that he was only there to work and there was otherwise little interest in him.

Although nothing can bring Cyril Pustan back to life or restore the loss to his family, friends, colleagues, and students, I believe that some conclusions can be drawn from the events and situations described above. Perhaps in this way a future similar tragedy can be avoided.

I would be grateful for a personal answer."

She added on 16 September 1977 that;

"I would like to add a few things to the list of items that I sent you yesterday.

With regard to the training in educational television he undertook in England and which he was unable to apply on his return to Jena, it was a blow to his self-confidence to find out later that someone else was sent to the television centre in Halle several times a month for training. Nothing was said to Cyril about this, and he had no further contact with the educational television. It was as if he had never taken the course.

Regarding the editing of translations, it can be said that most of the manuscripts required almost more translation than editing since in most cases the authors were scientists who did the translations themselves with the help of a dictionary. There were some cases of real editing, manuscripts whose authors had cooperated with him since he started working at the university, whose terminology and style he knew, and whose English was of a high standard. He insisted on doing this out of personal friendship and never as a burden.

One point that I forgot to mention is the creative ambitions and talents that could have been very useful for the University, but which were not noticed or not promoted. When his book "British and American Songs" for which he had worked for a number of years was published by "Enzyklopädie" in 1971, there was no discussion with him, neither was there any suggestion to write anything else after these rich efforts. He was always interested in writing, and he wrote well. But his lack of German prevented him writing in German or attending an amateur writers' circle.

He acquired knowledge of photography and did excellent colour slides and black and white photos. He went to the University

147

Photo Club a couple of times but again his lack of German made it difficult for him to take advantage of it. He loved music and took singing and guitar lessons which his students took advantage of while learning songs. If the university gave him support, he could have built an English choir and drama club but there was no interest."

The University Response

Professor Erich Leitel, who was the head of the Foreign Language Department, replied that Cyril did not raise the issues now complained of by Regina, and;

Cyril was *"always treated with courtesy, respect, and generosity... he was repeatedly advised not to take on too much...*

Mr Pustan was an introverted man who found contact with other people with difficulty. An eccentric (including vegetarian). The reasons for his lack of contact are by no means to be found in the allegedly inadequate language skills. It was also difficult to get into conversation with him in English. Englishmen working in the GDR also told me that he had hardly any contact with them and that it had been difficult to have a conversation with him. I was even asked what kind of "weird guy" we had. As far as I know he was therefore only invited once to the MHF International College English course and never again.

In 1975/76 he spent 9 months in England where he underwent a bladder operation with difficult follow up treatment. That put a lot of strain on him...He repeatedly hesitated to move into the apartment assigned to him in May 1976. Instead of going on vacation and resting, he prepared a lecture about the gymnastics and sports festival, went to Leipzig, ...and undertook the exertions of the gruelling trip to England while he was supposed to give lectures. At the same time the semester began with its requirements. Already in 1975 he had attempted suicide (we only now become aware of this)...

Mr Pustan has repeatedly, albeit with interruptions on his travels to England, received German lessons. This is shown by the independent written timetable of the FS 1977. He was even given English lessons. A stay at the Herder Institute was out of the question for him as it is well known that the Institute only prepares beginners who come directly from abroad for admission to the degree. After they have acquired initial knowledge, they then receive German lessons at the universities where they are studying. Mr Pustan had the opportunity to take part in courses for foreigners with us, and of course in all courses in German studies. He has partly done what Mrs Fischer confirms. Progress in the German language was only impaired by his month long stays in England (3 months 1971, 10 months 1971 to 1972, 9 months 1976).

In addition, he made too little use of the German language he had acquired, practised too little and had not sought conversations on his own initiative. His knowledge of German was sufficient, the only thing missing was practise. After all he was alive for 15 years in the GDR and thus in a German speaking environment. In this respect, the fact that he only spoke English to his wife at home was a disadvantage...Mrs Fischer...did not help him to learn the German language either...

His schedule shows that he taught regional studies and phonetics...

His housing problem did not become known until 1975. He had not told us about it. He was then put in front of other urgent cases and suggested a new apartment in Khala. He refused this however which caused considerable relief among his colleagues, especially those seeking accommodation. The reason he gave was that he could not expect his wife to climb the 4 flights of stairs. He had not moved into another apartment shown to him in May 1976 by his death on 8 September 1977."

Victor and Lutz had both heard a rumour that Cyril had committed suicide. The family knew that Cyril was very upset at him feeling he had to go back to Germany. They were unaware of the turbulence in his life.

And what was Cyril's secret?

Not only did he become friends with the teacher from the Music and Art School in Jena, but he married her on 13 July 1977.

Regina in her letter of 15 September 1977 had written that Cyril and Lieselotte were due to move into the new apartment in Jena when he died *"but the delay had been caused by her illness and surgical treatment."* In relation to his trips around July 1977 to fix his camera equipment using a workers' rail card, Professor Leitel wrote that *"Since his current wife was in hospital in Weimar for an operation, that made his visits to her from Leipzig cheaper."* He added that there *"very serious private problems connected with his divorce from Mrs Fischer... He said he had been divorced from his former wife (Mrs Fischer) as she made him nervous, and he would have broken if he has not separated ...Although he had been divorced from Mrs Fischer for about 1 ½ years he still lived with her and not with his new wife."*

Professor Leitel noted the lack of complaint by Cyril, wondered what Regina did to help him cope, criticised her for not complaining then, wondered what role she played in his mental state, wondered what led to the divorce, wondered what happened after the divorce, wondered why they still shared the apartment after the divorce, wondered why Regina had encouraged him to drive to Leipzig to deal with his camera equipment when Lieselotte was in hospital in Weimar and wondered why he prepared an extensive trip to England instead of having a vacation and rest. He had previously said that employing Cyril as a lecturer in 1964 *"was a very generous decision as Mr Pustan was a plumber by profession and did not have the scientific prerequisites to teach at the University."*

One cannot help but wonder if Professor Leitel had read any of the references or testimonies supplied by the other academics. He plainly felt slighted by Regina's assertions. His poor-quality set of questions entirely miss the point that even on Professor Leitel's own account there was merit in the complaint about his accommodation, about his linguistic isolation, and about his wish to learn more so he could teach better. Blaming Regina for Cyril's problems was a lazy way out and did the University no favours.

Cyril was a quiet man and never complained, so why would he change his personality just because he was in Germany? As he had not learned German, he would have been even more isolated. He was not materialistic so why would he seek better accommodation? He cared for his wife so why would he want her to climb 4 flights or have to travel further to get to work? He wanted to integrate so why would he not seek to learn German? He wanted to be the best teacher he could, so why would he not seek to do additional courses?

The robust response, tone, and lack of empathy for this kind, generous, hardworking man who never complained about his lot, may give an indication that the assertions made by Regina had merit.

And neither Regina nor Professor Leitel factored in that Cyril had required a prostatectomy and hospitalisation and recuperation for lengthy periods which may have been a significant factor affecting his mental health.

Lieselotte

Lieselotte (sometimes spelt Liselotte) Goring was born on 18 February 1933. Her parents were Otto Edmund Goring who was born in 1885 and died when Lieselotte was 7 in 1940, and Anna who was born in 1902. She had 4 siblings. She was a musician who played and wrote classical sheet music for the flute and recorder, had a booklet published called "Die Altbockflöte

Ein Schulwerk" (The alto recorder. A school work) and was a Doctor of Philosophy. She also conducted the Student Choir on his record. She later moved to teach the recorder at the Hochschule für Musik "Franz Liszt" Weimar for many decades. Cyril had known Lieselotte for a number of years and had given her a musicians' diary in 1972. Lieselotte was not Jewish.

Lieselotte

Annegret Fischer was a pupil of Lieselotte from 1987-1992, who also coached her in the recorder in 1995/1996. Annegret remembers Lieselotte as a gentle, warm-hearted, brilliant-minded person with a fine sense of humour and a very wide mental and intellectual horizon. Lieselotte had also some melancholy about her which she did not show Annegret much since Annegret was a child when they first met. Later Annegret heard from other people that Lieselotte had lost her quite newly-married husband, but she would never talk to Annegret about him. Lieselotte said or wrote to Annegret once; *"Das Leben ist ein einziges Abschiednehmen"* which gives some insight how she must have felt as it means *"life is a single farewell"*.

Lieselotte died on 14 October 2004. She was buried on 26
November 2004.

Cyril's headstone was updated to include Lieselotte. It was paid
for by her family and is maintained by her nephew, Hans-Christof
Kaiser. Each year a candle is lit on 8 September in his memory by
a Jewish friend of the family, Elizabeth.

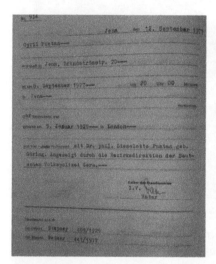

The women in Cyril's life in Germany at
his funeral Lieseolotte, Christine, Regina

לזכר נשמת
ר׳ שעפטל בן ר׳ חיים יהודה אריה
נפטר כ׳׳ו אלול תשל׳׳ז
CYRIL PUSTAN (PUSTANSKY)
DIED 8th SEPTEMBER 1977

לזכר נשמת
האשה העֿנא מלכה בת ר׳ מאיר
נפטרה כ׳׳ו אלול תשל׳׳ב
ANNIE SAFFER
DIED 5th SEPTEMBER 1972

The Yahrzeit Plaque at the Beth Hamedrash
Hagadol Synagogue in Leeds

The anniversary of Cyril's death in the Hebrew calendar is the same as my grandmother's, 26 Ellul. Their plaques are displayed together.

Was Cyril a spy?

The theory considered in Harald's paper that Regina was a Russian spy seems to fly in the face of an understanding of how the Stasi worked. The same applies when considering whether Cyril was a spy as well.

The Stasi was one of the most effective and repressive intelligence agencies ever to exist. It worked closely with the KGB. It spied on its population primarily through a vast network of citizens turned informants and arrested 250,000 people as political prisoners.

Cyril would have been arrested by the Stasi if they had even the slightest inkling he was a spy for MI6, the British Foreign Intelligence Service. The Stasi conducted spying operations abroad.

I very much doubt the theory considered by Harald in part due to Regina's propensity to move around, her lack of stability, and the numerous internships, courses, and short-term jobs she did throughout her time in Jena. Whether she was a spy or not, there is a file in the Stasi archive on both her and Cyril, they being foreign nationals.

What possible secrets could Cyril find out for them on his trips to London where he did some short courses, had medical treatment, and spent time with family? He had no connections to the British government. He had no access to anyone of influence. He was a plumber turned English language lecturer. Whilst Esther thought the phone was tapped when Cyril and Regina came to stay, he was never arrested and she was never accused of espionage by MI5, the British Secrity Service. Ella said that he was searched whenever he went to East Germany and was asked why he was going there. And Hans-Christof remembers that both Cyril and Lieselotte were well aware of being under surveillance.

The possibility of him being a double agent is even more fanciful, even though that may explain his lack of arrest by one side or the other. Of course, spies are supposed to fit in and not be seen, but the lifetime behaviour identifies Cyril as a hardworking, principled, honourable man. He was simply a man with Communist ideals and a love of his family in the United Kingdom that he would not have betrayed for anything. He was not interested in material well being. He could not be bought. He did not hate either side in the Cold War. He just preferred a more equal society and wanted peace.

And when was he trained? There are no gaps in this CV for "Spy School".

The closest one could come in asserting that Cyril helped "the enemy" was that he taught scientists to speak and understand English better. This enabled them to better understand papers written in English and be better able to communicate with their counterparts. He also explained about British society as he saw it through his discussions of life in Britan and analysis of the British press.

I think it is extremely unlikely Cyril or Regina spied for anyone. Whilst they were very much on the left of the political spectrum and had views that were not supported by the British or American establishment, that does not mean they were not patriotic.

And so why was Uncle Cyril the plumber who saved the world?

Cyril believed in peace and brotherhood, was active in promoting it, was willing to fly in the face of public and family opinion to promote it, and challenged those in power to achieve it. He was one of those who was the conscience of the world. Given Cyril's world view of peace and brotherhoood, his actions of helping people understand each other better helped reduce misunderstanding, enabled knowledge to be shared, and made the world a safer place. He was great fun, modest, quiet, unassuming, and a truly lovely man. Cyril had no children, but left behind loving relatives, and a legacy of striving for peace, reconciliation, and social justice. He worked hard and used his intellect to benefit others.

It says in the Jerusalem Talmud in Sanhedrin Chapter 4 verse 5, that *"whoever saves a life, it is considered as if he saved an entire world"*. I think that by Cyril's actions in concert with all the other peace activists with whom he marched, walked, and protested, he made political and military leaders stop and think, and helped prevent bloodshed. In accordance with the Jewish principles engrained in him, by saving a single life, Uncle Cyril was The Plumber who Saved the World.

He will now be remembered each year on 26 Ellul when his Yahrzeit (memorial) candle will be lit by Sally, his Yahrzeit plaque is lit at the Beth Hamedrash Hagadol Synagogue in Leeds, and Kaddish is said for him as is the Jewish custom. And he is remembered by you having read this account of his life.

Cyril Pustan, the plumber who saved the world

Annex

The San Francisco to Moscow Walk for Peace gets there!

Late in November 1960, six men and two women drove from New York City to San Francisco. Driving day and night, changing drivers as they went, the group sped through the land, straight through the first big blizzard of the year in Wyoming, came safely through a sudden tyre blow out near Reno, Nevada, and hurried through the sunshine and flowering landscape of California to the rendezvous in San Francisco.

What had brought these people together, most of whom were strangers to each other, and why had they crossed the continent with such speed and determination? They had come to start a walk for peace that would last over ten months and take them over two continents and an ocean to Moscow, capital of the Soviet Union.

Why in this machine age and especially in America, a country on wheels did the group want to walk? Because walking is basic to all mankind. By taking upon themselves such a task, with all the hardship and sacrifice it would entail, the group hoped to underline to the world their deep concern about the danger of destruction of the human race itself and to arouse individuals to themselves undertake direct action for peace - to act to put an end to the arms race, to ban nuclear weapons for ever, and to adopt non-violent methods of settling differences between nations.

Who were the people that finally marched into Red Square in Moscow on October 3, 1961? There were nine women and 22 men. The group arranged from a 19 year old youngster to a 48 year old grandmother. Americans made up half of the group, the others coming from England, France, the German Federal Republic, Norway, Sweden, Belgium and Finland. Religious backgrounds included Unitarian, Roman Catholic, Jewish, Quaker, Lutheran, Christian Scientist, and Mennonite, as well as atheist and agnostic. Among the marchers were a professional model, a plumber, an anthropologist, an aeroplane design engineer, a secretary, a nurse, a teacher, an actor, a chemist, and a medical student. The group itself was independent of any political or religious affiliations.

The peace walk was first conceived and organised by the Committee for Nonviolent Action (CNVA), 158 Grand Street, New York 13, New York. This is a group of about 60 Americans of differing political, religious and racial composition, living in all parts of the country. First organised in 1957, the purpose of the CNVA is to sponsor direct actions of protest and demonstration against American military power and policies. Among CNVA's members and followers, a number have gone to prison for civil disobedience - that is, for deliberately breaking laws which they believe it is essential to break as part of such protests.

In 1957, 11 persons trespassed illegally on the construction site of a missile base in the western state of Nevada. Others lay down on the road to prevent trucks from bringing materials to a missile site near Omaha, Nebraska; one man was run over by a truck.

The world-famous voyage of the 30 ft. ship Golden Rule in 1958 was another CNVA project. It was sent toward America's Pacific Ocean bomb's testing zone with a crew of four CNVA members. This voyage aroused millions of people to protest further against American bomb tests. George Willoughby, one of the four crewmen, was among the marchers that entered Red Square.

CNVA took part in the 1959 international protest against the French bomb tests in the Sahara, operating from a base in Ghana. Sustained demonstrations by CNVA against America's Polaris missile submarines have involved hundreds of people since the summer of 1960 in the eastern seaboard area of the New London, Connecticut shipyards.

At the rally in San Francisco's historic Union Square two more joined, making it ten to start the walk. More than half of these finished in New York. In between, literally thousands have walked with the team for periods ranging from a few hours in the vicinity of the large cities to periods of several months. Many thousands more have attended meetings held en route. Millions around the globe have heard members of the walk speak on the radio, seen them on television, or read of them in newspapers. That first day will not be forgotten by the walkers. The heavens seemed to open, soaking everyone to the skin. Their new boots squelched water at every step. That night ten exhausted people lay in their sleeping bags amid a litter of sodden boots, packs and clothing on the floor. The walk was on its way.

The peace walk followed along the main highways east carrying large signs reading "San Francisco to Moscow Walk for Peace," "End the Arms Race - Let Mankind Live," "Unilateral Disarmament - a Call to East and West," "Act for Peace – Refuse to Work in Defence Industries," "Act for Peace - Refuse to Serve in the Armed Forces," "Act for Peace – Refuse to Pay Taxes for Military Purposes," "Trust in God, not in SAC," and many more.

The signs were oilcloth on board, and were constantly being broken, torn or just worn out. New ones were continually being made by one of the walkers, Millie Gilbertson, a commercial artist from New Jersey who had been active in Polaris Action during the summer of 1960.

We averaged 25 miles (40 km.) a day from San Francisco to Chicago, about 20 miles a day from Chicago to New York. In the heavily populated eastern half of the country more people walked with us and many more meetings were held, so the pace was kept down.

Much depended on what sleeping and eating arrangements could be made each day and on the number and location of *whatever public meetings could be arranged, if any. An advance team of one or two members went ahead in a little DKW car loaned to us in California to scout out these arrangements. Most nights the walkers slept in their sleeping bags on the floor of the first church willing to take them. Those were the good nights: during the approximately six weeks it took us to cross the far western states from eastern Arizona to the midwest, we had to sleep out on the road about 20 nights. Shelter was hard to find for such unpopular ideas in these areas.*

Food was often provided by local sympathisers, especially in California and western Arizona, then again starting in the state of Kansas and going on to the eastern seaboard. Most frequently we could count on hospitality from Quakers, the Church of the Brethren, Mennonites and Methodists, but we stayed overnight in at least a hundred churches of practically all different denominations before we got to New York. We also slept in Salvation Army hostels, community centres, private homes and a jail.

All along the route many people gave the walkers food, lodging, or money. One lady stopped her car on the highway in California and gave one of the girls a handkerchief and a roll of toilet paper, a most welcome present! This lady, whose name we never thought to ask, also predicted we would be well treated in the Soviet Union, which she said she had recently visited. At that time there were several in our group who believed we might well be shot at the Russian border for trying to cross over.

Once, a truck driver drove up to us and handed a walker a twenty-dollar bill. Then he said "You're doing more for peace than I am," and drove off without telling us his name.

CNVA had a mailing list of about 3,000 people to whom it regularly sent reports of its Polaris Action or other current projects, and from whom it received contributions of one, two, sometimes five or 10 dollars. As the walk progressed, the mailing list expanded to about 7,000 contributors. Collections were also made locally at meetings held by the walk. Some of the walkers themselves paid all or part of their own expenses.

We had the hardest time in the far western states of Arizona (the eastern part), New Mexico, Texas and Oklahoma. In these areas the towns are often 50 or 75 miles apart, with no sign of life for miles in between. In recent years the armed forces have built many rocket, missile and Air Force bases in these areas, perhaps because of the good climate and sparse population.

The constant construction of new bases in these areas offers the main source of employment. Many people saw the demands of the walkers as a threat to their jobs. Others believed it simply treacherous to demand that such bases be closed. The small town of Santa Maria, near the Arizona border of California, proudly displayed a large banner across its Main Street – "Missile Capital of the Western Hemisphere." It was located near Vandenberg Air Force Base, site of many missile experiments, where we also held a demonstration. In such areas few churches were willing to let us sleep on their floors.

An attempt was made to prevent us holding a scheduled meeting on the campus of Arizona State University in Tempe, Arizona, near Tucson. We heard later that the John Birch Society, a new organisation of fascist tendencies, was behind the attempt. About a mile before we got to the campus, a group of about 30 young men students came out on the highway and tried to stop us, saying we were "undesirables" and "not wanted".

It looked as if they might use force, regardless of the women in the group, but finally some of them began to defend our right to be heard. This took place after we had talked with them a while and urged that democracy should rule. Instead of the lunch hour meeting originally scheduled, over three hundred students came out to hear us and kept us with questions until 5p.m. when we had to leave for an evening supper and meeting.

One teacher created a sensation when he resigned his position on the Tempe faculty in order to join our march.

We held a 24-hour-vigil to commemorate Hiroshima's victims at Alamogordo, New Mexico. The vigil took place at the enormous White Sands Proving Grounds; the first atomic explosion history took place here, laying the groundwork for America's Hiroshima try-out.

Only one small Mexican church would agree to let us sleep in their nearby building. Soon the minister was visited by local police cars. Then he got a long distance call from the bishop of his Church, many miles away in El Paso, Texas, saying the peace walk could not sleep in the church. At last, late in the evening, one of his church members permitted us to spend the rest of the freezing-cold February night on an unused open lot he owned.

We were walking along the highway in Arizona one day in January 1961 when we were stopped by a car coming from Roswell, New Mexico, some weeks walk to the east. The driver told us that the officials of the Walker Strategic Air Command Base in Roswell had recently invited the ministers and other leading local citizens in Roswell to a dinner at the base. Therefore the request was made that we be given no hospitality, publicity, or cooperation.

When we arrived in Roswell some weeks later no church would put us up. Several citizens in responsible positions indicated - literally behind locked doors – that they would have liked to help but could not take the risk.

But the Salvation Army did take us in and kept us for two nights. While we were there the phone kept ringing with complaints about our being allowed to stay there but the Salvation Army officer stood firm. He maintained that he could not refuse shelter to any one homeless or destitute regardless of what ideas they might have!

We demonstrated before the gates of the SAC base in Roswell. We handed out leaflets to each car as it rolled up to the gate, and saw the sentry on duty demand and take back its leaflet as the cars passed him. A youngster of about 12 told Scott Herrick, who was there handing out leaflets and holding the sign, that his father had been an army chaplain at the base and had told him that the SAC base kept the Russians from coming and taking God away.

In February 1961 the United Press International News Agency carried a statement by the Federal Bureau of Investigation. The statement denied that the FBI had asked newspapers, radio or television stations to refuse publicity to the Walk for peace.

In a small town in Oklahoma, the local gas station man expressed his surprise to hear us speaking English. He said he had just that morning heard on the radio that a band of Russian communists was going to pass through the town on a so-called walk for peace. The local college had refused us permission to speak on their campus (Northwestern State Teachers College). None of the churches would put us up, so we set up beneath the bridge spanning the dry bed of a river about a mile out of town.

That night a group of students drove out to us from the college and came down to our camp fire carrying torches and signs saying "Workers arise! Stamp out thirst! Drink beer!" But they soon became serious, threw away the signs and torches, and stayed to discuss with us until 2:30 in the morning.

For many of these students it was the first they had heard expressed the thought that civil defence was a fraud, that the way to peace was through disarmament and not through ever greater military might, and there was such a thing possible as refusal to serve in the armed forces through a stand as a conscientious objector. The minister of a local church also came out with a few of his congregation and brought as popcorn and apples.

Amarillo is a large industrial city and we expected no difficulty in locating at least one church or college that would be interested in helping us arrange meetings and provide a place to sleep. But over one hundred telephone calls we made there were in vain; none of the major churches or schools would consider it. Only two churches permitted us to speak to their congregation, both Negro churches. One spontaneously collected several dollars for us. While sitting in this church an old Negro woman put her arms around me and gave me a kiss and thanked me. Next she searched through her pocket and handed me twenty cents.

While passing out leaflets in front of two military bases near Amarillo, three members of our team were arrested. Two had to pay outrageously high fines of 40 dollars 50 cents each and were told by the judge that they were "just no good." The local police picked up three members of the team who were distributing leaflets to soldiers on leave from the air base in the shopping center of downtown Amarillo. The police held and questioned them for an hour and the let them go to join the rest of the walk already out on the highway going east.

As we went east our reception became as friendly as it had been in San Francisco, Los Angeles and the other places in California. At the university town of Columbia, Missouri, different members of our group spoke at a total of 50 meetings during a period of three days.

We had a large public meeting on the campus of Washington University, St. Louis, Missouri, in March. Next day pickets appeared with signs protesting at our having been permitted on the campus. The third day Washington University students picketed in a counter demonstration. The nationally respected newspaper, the St Louis Post-Dispatch, carried front-page photos of these events for three days running. Three weeks later the students and local citizens joined forces to organise the first peace walk ever held in St Louis.

Many people joined us along the way for longer or shorter periods of time. One girl drove all the way from California to

Alamogordo a distance of about 1,000 miles (1600 km.). Russell Stabler of the department of mathematics in an eastern college went by train from New York to Oklahoma and back just to walk with us for four days during the Washington's Birthday long weekend. By the time we reached Chicago we had 18 permanent members.

In Chicago, the largest city in the midwest, we had many meetings and were received most hospitably. Radio and television interviewers stopped the marchers on the walk through the streets of Chicago. They also came to the Easter Sunday wedding of Beatrice Burnette and Scott Herrick, who had met in San Francisco the day they started on the walk. Later, another romance followed when Martha Rich, who left college to join the walk in Kansas, married Barton Stone from San Francisco.

Our walk joined forces with Chicago's own 50 mile Easter walk - much of it through snow and sleet. It wound up with a 2,000 strong rally in the city's centre addressed by A.J Muste and the well-known nuclear scientist William Davidon. Soon after leaving Chicago the walk had grown to 35 members.

The team passed through such industrial centres as Toledo, Ohio, and Pittsburgh, Pennsylvania, where it demonstrated in the street in spite of a Civil Defence mock air raid. Then we walked over the Alleghany mountains, through the Cumberland Gap of the old covered wagon trail and into the state of Maryland. The team held an all-day vigil before the gates of Fort Detrick, Maryland, notorious as the centre of American military research into bacteriological warfare. Here too the sentry on guard took back the leaflets we had just given to the cars as they came in.

In the nation's capital the Quakers arranged many meetings and lavish hospitality for the team. We visited the White House early in May and talked with Arthur Schlesinger Jr., one of President Kennedy's advisors. He disagreed thoroughly with the team's proposal that the United States should disarm unilaterally

*regardless of what the Soviet Union or any other nation does, but
he did wish us well.*

*The team held a 75-hour protest demonstration in relays day and
night in front of the Pentagon in Washington. When Andrews Air
Force Base in Washington D.C. held its huge celebration for
Armed Forces Day, members of the team also visited it and
distributed 10,000 leaflets against military armaments.*

*Individuals on the team joined the picket line in front of the
Central Intelligence Building in Washington to protest against
CIA intervention in Cuba.*

*In the latter part of May the team came to Philadelphia. There
the Quakers provided generous hospitality for the team and held
many large meetings at which substantial donations were given
to the team for its European expenses. Hundreds walked with us
in the hot sun. Many were families with baby carriages.*

*We walked into the city of New York at the end of May and held
the ceremony before the United Nations headquarters. At the
final send-off for Europe, an honoured guest was Jim Peck of the
CNVA executive committee, just back from a "freedom ride" on a
bus protesting against racial segregation in the southern states.
He had 56 stitches in his face and head from a severe beating the
mob had given him.*

*It was originally planned to send five to ten of the team to
Europe, but eventually 17 Americans were able to go. At least
10,000 people contributed money to send them. A number
of those who remained behind joined the Polaris Action
demonstrations in New London, and some of those were later to
go to prison for their part in the demonstrations.*

*On the morning of June 1 we swooped by plane into London
amidst excited shouts of "That must be the Thames!" "Where's
the Tower of London?" and people sliding back and forth across*

seats and aisles to get a view of the other side. Soon we had landed and piled out. My ears were popping, and it was raining.

We remarked on the clean streets, and the houses looking so different from ours, the bright flower gardens, and emerald-green grass. The roofs seem crowded with odd -looking things that look like flower pots. We were surprised to learn they were chimneys leading from fireplaces in each room.

The San Francisco to Moscow Walk for Peace has now become the American-European March strengthened by British and European team members. We hold many meetings to hammer out our future plans. We shop for equipment we will need in England and on the Continent. We have numerous public meetings, including a large one at the Friends Meeting House Euston Road. Finally, on June 4, we get an enthusiastic send-off from 6,000 at the rally in London's famous Trafalgar Square.

Standing high up on the plinth under Lord Nelson, we fight a losing battle with the pigeons calmly roosting above our heads. We look out into a sea of faces and banners. It is a thrilling moment. For the first time we can actually see and hear that there are really people - many people - who take us seriously and back us up. Although we have just left America, we feel this is a true homecoming.

The Campaign for Nuclear Disarmament first publicly established its policy of serious attention and support for the march at Trafalgar Square. The popular support thus crystallised in England was decisive, I am certain, in insuring that the march received permission to enter the countries of the East.

CND support brought out thousands to walk with the peace marchers to the outskirts of London. CND organisations continued to draw crowds, bring newspaper, radio and television publicity, and arrange public meetings, large and small all along the route of our 50-mile walk to Southampton. Many times the hospitality and meetings were arranged with the Quakers. Along the route we had factory-gate and village-green meetings. A vigil was held at Aldermaston, the Atomic Weapons Research Establishment, which has become the goal each Easter of the British marchers for peace.

As we arrived in Southampton we got word from A.J. Muste in Moscow that the Russians had agreed to let us in and that he would now visit Poland and East Germany to get their permission. All through our walk in the United States the most frequent question had been, "do you really think the Communists will let you in?" It was not to be Russia but our own ally, France, that refused us.

The Friends Meeting House in Southampton was crowded when we said farewell before sailing on the British Railways channel steamer Normannia. But when we arrived in Le Havre on the morning of June 13, we were flatly refused permission to land. No reason was forthcoming, and finally, after notifying all the authorities, we held a protest demonstration in which four members of the team jumped overboard and swam ashore to distribute leaflets and speak briefly to the French people, while a fifth man jumped and remained on shore. The four who were rounded up by the police and returned to the ship persisted in their demonstrations, jumped overboard again, and again were returned to the ship. On our second attempt a week later, on June 22, France again refused us entry and this time 19 of our group went over the side of the ship. All were again returned to England by the French authorities.

Newspaper photographers and television cameras recorded our protest in the waters of Le Havre. We hoped that in this way many people all over the world would realise how important it was to us - and to them - to raise the demand for an end to the arms race before the people of every nation, without Government interference. A BBC television man later told us that the French government's intransigence had resulted in more people

169

throughout the world learning about the San Francisco to Moscow peace marchers than if we had been granted permission to enter.

It was only later that we learned that the French government notified British Railways in advance that we would not be admitted to France.

Although we were denied entrance, a group of French pacifists carried out our peace walk for us in France. Their signs and leaflets were several times confiscated, and finally they used signs that were sewed or tied to their clothing. We met them at the Belgian border point of Courtrai on July 2 and then resumed our peace walk through Belgium according to the regular schedule. While waiting for the French team we laid drainage pipes and cleared away underbrush at a farm near Rummen, Belgium, to help prepare it for service as an international peace center.

In Belgium we had the help of the Catholic Church for the first time. We ate and slept at many Catholic schools, convents and monasteries. A young Catholic priest, Abbe Carrette of Charleroi, accompanied us on foot and helped arrange hospitality and public meetings. Our outdoor meetings were held in the market places with the aid of our truck and loud-speakers going before us announcing them. Our indoor meetings were generally arranged in local coffeehouses or cafe's, in keeping with the local custom.

Many Quakers and members of the War Resisters' International walked with us in Belgium. Meetings of several hundred persons were held in Brussels and Antwerp. We demonstrated before NATO headquarters in Brussels, and before the National Fabrique des Armes.

On July 16 we entered the Federal Republic of Germany at Aachen. Many peace groups helped us in Germany - the German Peace Union, Quakers, War Resisters' International, Hamburg

Non-violent Resistance Group, Women's peace groups and a few trade unions. We slept and ate in youth hostels, private homes, houses of the Friends of Nature, Quaker meeting houses, and at the International Friendship House in Buekenburg, near Hanover.

Police escorts accompanied the march practically all the time; sometimes the police cars carried our rucksacks for some when we became tired. We had quite a few disagreements with the police over the slogans we could carry, which they felt had to be approved in writing every time. We also had some differences with the police when they re-routed the walk so it would not pass by military barracks or other military installations lying directly on the route. We tried very hard to obtain official permission to hold military protest demonstrations in West Germany but could not succeed.

Therefore on August 3 we arranged four simultaneous demonstrations against the War Ministry in Bonn, the Bergenhohne NATO military base, the Dortmund Brackell rocket base, and the Hanover recruiting headquarters. The police did not permit the Dortmund and Bonn demonstrations to be carried out as planned. Some of the demonstrators were arrested briefly, tried, and sentenced to brief sentences or fines, none of which were carried out.

Many Germans, usually between 50 and 60 at a time, walked with us along our route, especially on weekends. About 200 walked with us on August 6 through Braunschweig to a memorial service in the centre of the town for the Hiroshima dead. The procession, with signs demanding banning of atom bombs and bearing black flags, was most solemn and impressive.

Some spoke of how their thinking had undergone a long and painful change after their wartime experiences and the catastrophes that had finally put an end to the war. I felt it was a tribute to the essential goodness of people that these men today were sincere partisans of peace and could no longer support the military policies of their country.

171

The group of marchers who took part in the Bergenhohne demonstration also visited the site of the notorious Belsen concentration camp nearby. Everything has long been cleared away; the sole evidence that this was once an extermination centre where 50,000 Russian war prisoners and 30,000 others, mostly Jews, perished, is a number of mounds of earth bearing granite plaques. The plaques indicate the number of dead - 500 here, 2,500 there, 800 here, 5,000 there - obviously rough approximations of the carnage. Only granite memorials and a few scattered gravestones now testify to the human suffering that took place there during the war.

While we were looking at these graves we could hear sounds like thunder coming from the Bergenhohne shooting ranges all around the areas. Giant-size tanks were seen travelling along the roads. Planes and helicopters were overhead constantly. Truckloads of soldiers were coming and going. The terrible message of Belsen was it seemed, being lost in the confusion.

On August 2 we crossed the border from Helmstedt to Marienborn in the German Democratic Republic. We were given a very friendly reception from the German Peace Council and found many people waiting to greet us. During our brief visit to the GDR great trouble was taken to provide us with good food, convenient places to sleep and opportunities to talk to people accompanying us on the walk or at public meetings or along the road.

Practically all the people expressed their horror of war, a desperate desire for peace and a deep fear that they might be attacked. All made clear their desire for a peace treaty which would demilitarise the whole area of Germany on both sides and which would guarantee that no former Nazi leader would ever again hold positions of leadership in West Germany. Their fears and desires seemed to be reasonable and based on realities. At no time did anyone express desire for revenge or any wish to force their way of life on West Germany.

We carried our signs and distributed our leaflets everywhere just as we had done in the West. 15,000 leaflets were distributed in the week we spent in the GDR.

Unfortunately for us we came to Berlin just at the moment of the Berlin crisis - August 14, 1961. We were told that we would not be permitted to enter Berlin but could go by bus toward the Polish border, there to resume our walk.

Three members of the team accepted this proposal as reasonable under the extraordinary circumstances. The rest of the team refused, feeling it was their first duty as a non-violent group to go where the danger of violence was the greatest, and believing that their presence might alleviate the Berlin situation. Although the team was not aware of it yet, the authorities in West Berlin had also decided to refuse permission for the team to march with signs or leaflets in West Berlin. Finally, the team was put on a bus and taken back to Helmstedt on the West German border.

After several days of discussion between A.J. Muste and the Peace Councils of the GDR and Poland, it was agreed that the march could proceed to Poland. The GDR Peace Council provided transit visas and a bus so that on August 22 the team was reunited in Poland. The three who had refused to return to West Germany awaited the others at the border point.

From the moment of our arrival in Poland we felt that it was here we were receiving the warmest welcome of our entire trip. From the time we crossed the Oder river to our approach to the eastern border the Polish Peace Committee gave us unfailing courtesy, genuine friendliness and strenuous efforts to help us meet as many people as possible. Polish hospitality was far beyond anything we could have expected. The food was wonderful - often too plentiful and too good for our own good. We slept in beds every night, a record never equalled in America or anywhere else in Western Europe. Villagers invited us into their homes and asked us to let them hear from us in future. People met us all along the route with great interest. Students and teachers alike invited us into their classrooms to tell them about our efforts for peace.

A visit to Auschwitz made a profoundly saddening and terrifying impression. Auschwitz was far off our march route but at our special request the Polish Peace Council arranged for us to make a special trip there and back.

The Poles gave us complete freedom of speech on the streets and on the radio. We handed out leaflets and carried our signs everywhere without question or interference. No effort whatever was made to add their own signs or leaflets. Every effort was made to organise public meetings for us. At any time we were free to speak to people, visit them in their homes, go to movies, theatre, shopping or do any of the things anyone might do visiting abroad. No police accompanied the walk. We demonstrated freely before the Ministry of Defence in Warsaw.

Our relationships with the Polish Peace Committee were exceptionally cordial. Actually the walk's message is quite different from the Polish Peace Committee's beliefs, but that did not prevent them from doing all they could to help the walk state its views to the Polish people.

As we approached the border of Russia and it became time to say goodbye we felt sorry to leave Poland and wondered what it would be like in the last country of our route before returning home – the Soviet Union.

On the morning of September 15, a Saturday, we crossed the border from Poland into Russia. There was a long delay while we had to wait on the bridge over the Bug River between the two countries. The Soviets had resumed bomb-testing and our time in the USSR had been cut from six weeks to three weeks. We did not know how things would be in the USSR after the overflowing friendliness, freedom and hospitality of Poland.

All of a sudden the wind came up, it got cold, and it began to pour. We felt dismal enough. But the rain stopped, we were given a signal to come through the barrier, and before we knew it we were being met by photographers, people were handing us bouquets of gladioli, and we were being ushered into a building that looked more like a private house than a border customs point.

Nobody bothered to look in our baggage. The room was crowded with representatives of the press, radio and TV, as well as the Mayor of Brest himself, and many officials of Soviet peace organisations, Intourist, and others. Actually, the Soviet welcoming committee was ready and anxious to get us started with dinner and a visit to the Brest Fortress nearby. But the walkers would not budge until a long list of their questions was gone over. The meeting must have stretched out for three or four hours, wearing us all out. The Russians politely starved while we munched away on buns and sandwiches thoughtfully provided for us in advance by our Polish hosts.

Finally satisfied with the results of our negotiations, we all got up to start the march in the USSR.

Our walk went along in lovely weather to the famed Brest Fortress on the Bug River en route to the city of Brest. This fortress was one of the earliest casualties of the Nazi invasion. Completely cut off, the defenders held out for a month down to almost the last man, only a small handful escaping through the lines. The museum showed photographs, inscriptions scratched on pieces of stone preserved from the fortress saying, "We will die but not surrender," flags buried by the defenders and dug up intact years later, charred notebooks, clothing and photos, pieces of brick with surfaces fused from the heat of flame throwers, and other evidence of the struggle. Our guides explained that their personal experiences with the Nazis at that time caused them to fear and expect similar attacks in the future from those Nazis still in the Adanaeur government. The museum showed photographs and documents signed by the present Adanaeur officials when they were commanding officers in the Brest attacks.

That evening, after a fabulous feast in the Bug Hotel, replete with caviar and wine, not to mention vodka, we went to our first public meeting in the Soviet Union. The Trade Union House was packed. About 500 sat in seats, with many more crowding the doors and the hall.

A typical buxom blonde young Russian told how, when she was 15, she had seen Fascists drive people into houses and set fire to them, then throw children into the flames. She added, "I have four children now. I want to see their happiness with my own eyes. Millions of Soviet mothers and others in the world are worried about the young generation. We approve the peaceful policies of our government."

The walkers then spoke telling their reason for being on the walk. Bradford Lyttle, chief co-ordinator and organizer of the walk, brought the house down when he started the first major speech of the evening by saying in Russian, "Good evening, Russian friends." But he soon got cries of protest from the audience when he urged the Russians to refuse to serve in the armed forces, pay taxes for military use, or work in military industries.

When he said "I call on you to protest against bomb testing by your Government," he got indignant protests from the audience. He got murmurs of disbelief when he said that it was the American people's fear of Russian military power that makes the American Government and people arm and seek allies even among the Nazis in West Germany. However the audience applauded his courage in presenting his views against such opposition and his obvious sincerity in wanting to attain peace.

At another meeting, this time in a textile factory at Byeryeza in Byelorussia, Bradford stated: "Foreign countries believe that Russia attacked Finland (silence), Russia swallowed Czechoslovakia (laughter) and suppressed the revolution in Hungary"(cries of "We don't want to listen!" "Tell it to the

Americans!"). Bradford continued above the uproar, "These are hard words. I am just trying to tell you what Americans believe."

Since the distance from the border of Russia to Moscow was so great (658 miles, 1054 km.) and we had only three instead of six weeks to do it in, it became necessary to work out a shift system, somewhat similar to the one we used for a short time in the wider western expanses in the United States, only more intensive.

At first the Russians insisted we must stay together as a group, as we had actually agreed to do prior to our coming. To meet this requirement, and at the same time cover the mileage, meant that all the walkers had to get up at 4:45 in the morning, eat and get out on the road, there to remain until at least perhaps 10pm. in order to be able to say honestly that the entire distance had actually been walked by some part of the team. Soon the two buses accompanying us began to look like hospital ambulances. While part of the team walked, the others lay on seats and on the floor trying to catch up on a few hours sleep until their turn to relieve the others. Evening meetings and entertainments kept the walkers going until 2am or 3am and some hardly bothered to undress before they reeled into bed.

Soon the walkers began dropping like flies - picked up by the ambulances they were being taken to hospitals with exhaustion, indigestion and general disintegration. In alarm, the Russians called an emergency meeting with the group. They tried to dissuade the walkers, urging that they walk their usual approximately 40 km. (25 miles) each day as a single group and then take the bus the rest of the way to their destination for the night. In vain they pointed out that much of the route to Moscow lay through sparsely inhabited swampland and forest. The walkers remain determined - a walk was a walk and it must be walked. The Russians shook their heads over this, to them, quixotic attitude and gave in. Thereafter they cooperated in

*every possible way with a three shift system asked for by the team
starting at 3a.m. and finishing about 8p.m. enabling the team to
complete the walk to Moscow on foot.*

*In the three weeks we spent in the USSR, a conservative estimate
of the number of street meetings would be between one and two
hundred. The average would be at least 100 people, often several
hundreds to 1,000 or more. By comparison our meetings in the
United States or Western Europe averaged in the dozens, except
for the Trafalgar Square meeting of 6,000 and perhaps an
additional dozen large meetings reaching figures from 200 to
500, such as those in San Francisco, Los Angeles, St. Louis,
Chicago, Philadelphia, New York, Antwerp, and Braunschweig.*

*Spontaneous street meetings were almost unheard of in America,
somewhat more frequent in England, again rare in Western
Europe, and the regular order of things in the eastern countries.
They increased in size and frequency as we went further east. On
some days in populated areas in the Soviet Union as many as
eight or 10 meetings would be held one after the other along the
highway among the crowds gathering around the walkers.
Sometimes three or four meetings would be going on at once, the
number being limited only by the number of translators available
or the ability of the walker to make himself understood alone.
Sometimes walkers just started speaking to a few people and in
two seconds flat huge crowds were around.*

*The crowds were by no means mute spectators. Sometimes
people rushed up to a walker, hugged or kissed one, presented
flowers, shook hands or shouted, "Bravo ." One time a 14-year
old girl asked me in careful schoolroom English, "What is your
name?" with many giggles being exchanged between her and her
girl friend. She also gave me a little pottery squirrel. Another time
a girl gave a walker a ring, hugged her and exchanged addresses.*

*The Russians were not at all bashful about making speeches
themselves, often opposing strongly what the walkers had said.*

Often someone from the crowd asked questions or made replies. Some were heated or angry; others urged friendship between our countries. Some pleaded or demanded that we go back home and tell our people that the Russians had suffered enough during war and wanted only peace.

There were always plenty of translators around as the Russians provided us with three and we had our own, Patrick Proctor, a 6'5" young English art student from London. Occasionally local Russians could speak enough English, German or French for us to understand.

Crowds numbering up to a thousand or more sometimes gathered around the hotels or restaurants where we were stopping, to the point that it was next to impossible to get in or out. At Orsha the crowd had to be held back by a cordon, and at Gzhatsk I was cut off from the group by the crowd and had to appeal to a passerby to get me to the evening meeting where I was scheduled to be one of the groups speakers.

Speeches usually started around 8 or 9 pm and ended around 11 or 12pm, depending on whether our walkers came on time or were late. After the speeches came the entertainment, which could last until 1 or 2 in the morning. Local amateur talent might put on a dozen or more numbers, involving 20 to 100 persons, in programmes consisting of group or solo singing, recitations, ballet-dancing, folk-dancing, chamber music and individual performances.

In Russia, as in Poland, sleeping was always in beds. I do not recall having slept on the floor once in either country and had no more use for my sleeping bag. Sleeping bags on the floor were practically standard everywhere else, though in East Germany they also supplied us with mattresses. Most of the time in Russia we slept in hotels or schools, with fresh linen, blankets, and often, facilities for washing and laundry. At first we protested that beds were not necessary; we were used to roughing it and perfectly comfortable sleeping on floors. But our protests gradually grew feebler as we gratefully crawled into nice warm beds each night.

Medical care was always available and doctors appeared at the slightest whisper of a headache or upset stomach. A skin specialist and his nurse even appeared at 1am one night to apply ointment and bandage up the legs of a girl who had gotten a severe sun rash and blisters on an unexpectedly hot day. I myself also landed in a hospital in Minsk, the Rosa Luxembourg Fourth Clinical Hospital. I was taken there when I was suddenly seized with cramps and vomiting, and in a few days of treatment and rest recovered completely. While there I was much impressed by the friendly, informal relationship between the doctors, who were mainly women, the nurses and patients.

On September 30 we met the Gagarin family in the evening meeting at Gzhatsk. They sat on the stage with the chairman of the meeting. Gagarin's sister, a nurse in a children's institution, spoke at the meeting. She was quite indignant over the stress abroad on cosmic travel for military purposes and stressed that her brother's achievements in the conquest of space were great contributions to world science.

Our arrival in Moscow was a joyous occasion, the weather warm, sunny, just right. The streets were crowded with people, clapping, waving, some shaking our hands and thanking us, calling out to us, some in tears. Leaflets went like hotcakes.

We were surprised to see the broad, clean avenues, numerous speeding buses, the huge size of the housing developments everywhere, the crowded stores, and the floods of billboards advertising all kinds of plays, concerts, lectures, recitations, amateur talent programmes, and so on.

Our actual walk into Red Square and two hour demonstration there with our signs and leaflets were the high spot of our arrival.

Dozens of foreign and Soviet correspondents, plus radio and television, recorded the scene as crowds milled about, asked us questions, pressed all kinds of badges on us and asked for ours in return. I could hardly believe that we had actually made it - that after all these months of walking we had really reached our goal. It was a wonderful feeling. The job was done, and well done.

Some of the people in the crowd did not understand our silent vigil and kept trying to talk to us the whole time. One lady went about plaintively asking everybody why she was not being given a leaflet when she could plainly see that others had done. Some passed us notes, hoping that if we would not talk we could at least read. But they all had to wait until our silent vigil ended when the Kremlin Clock chimed 4 and the San Francisco to Moscow Walk for Peace was officially over.

Some days later I met a lovely young girl on a bus who told me she was a senior student in geology from Siberia. Her class had been given 140 rubles each from the school toward the cost of this combined vacation and field trip, which had taken them to the Crimea and the Caucasus in the far south. I told her we were with the San Francisco to Moscow Walk for Peace and she knew all about it already, had seen it on television and read about us in the papers. People on the bus were starting to listen and coming round to ask questions, but it was our stop to get off. We parted the best of friends.

I visited Novo-Alyesksyevsky church in Moscow on Sunday morning but could not get inside through the solid wall of worshippers, some of whom were standing outside singing the responses as the services went on inside. I had a similar experience in Opalencia, Poland, where people were standing six deep taking part in the services and it was barely possible to look in and see the gold adornments, beautiful pictures and statues everywhere, and the crowds inside.

The Moscow State University visit proved to be one of the highlights of the stay in Moscow. Very lively and free discussions took place both in the large amphitheatre for the scheduled meeting with about 200 students and all over the building in small groups gathered around various walkers, who were going about distributing leaflets and talking to students at will. The discussions ran so far over time that another important meeting, to which well-known public figures had been invited, had to be cancelled.

Hundreds of students argued back and forth with the marchers. Opinions were freely exchanged. Two students passed notes up to the walkers encouraging them. In the main, however, the students appeared to feel that unilateral disarmament was not going to be accepted by either the United States or the Soviet Union. They therefore urged more pressure for joint agreement on disarmament, under strict control, and a peace treaty with Germany. It was clear that in spite of differences of opinion, the Russians respected the marchers for their sincere desire for peace and their efforts on the march, and that the Russians supported the march as an expression of this desire for peace.

The meeting began at 10 in the morning with a speech by a Moscow State University Professor of chemistry who is also Vice-Provost of the University. His talk lasted about 20 minutes. He mentioned that among the 32,000 student body there were a total of 2,100 foreign students at the university, all of whom came under Government exchange agreements. There were 20 Americans, 30 British and 100 Chinese, among others. Then followed a brief tour of the geological museum. At about 11 o'clock the walkers were taken to a meeting with students in a large lecture hall. About 30 students and a small sprinkling of university staff were present. Students were constantly coming and going as their schedule of studies required; the amphitheatre gradually filled up during the speeches, so that the room contained about 100 or 150 students by the time the meeting ended.

First to speak was Bradford Lyttle, who gave the walk's full program for unilateral disarmament and non-violent resistance. Leafleting was going on in the lecture room and the halls by the other walkers, some of whom left to wander about the building and have informal meetings with students wherever they happened to meet them.

Professor Surunov, Professor of Philology, then gave a detailed refutation of non-violent resistance, saying it was non-violent only in a physical sense but not intellectually. He maintained that non-violent resistance to the Nazis would only have intensified their efforts against the population. Scott Herrick, one of the walk's participants and organizers, countered by saying that it was time to seek new ways to settle disputes between nations. If one was projecting slides on a wall and the colours came out distorted, he said, it was necessary to get a new slide.

A postgraduate student in the faculty of law said that the existence of American bases on European soil was contrary to international law. Several of the students also spoke briefly from the audience, without bothering to introduce themselves.

A West German team member then stated he could see no difference between the attitude of West Germany on their military policy and the attitude of the Soviet Union. West Germany said its policy was necessary, otherwise they were unable to defend their standard of living; although the Russians do have a desire for peace, that attitude was basically the same. This speech caused a stir in the audience. Professor Surunov leaped up and said he thought it offensive and presumptuous of his friend from West Germany to make any comparison between attitudes of the West German revenge-seekers and the Soviet people.

At this point Bradford Lyttle made an impassioned speech which in essence was intended as a plea for objectivity and seemed to have a deep effect on the audience. Notes kept coming up to Bradford every so often, some of them questions. Two criticised

*the law student's talk and tended to give Bradford support,
although qualifying it by saying unilateral disarmament was not
a realistic possibility.*

*The chairman then suggested that the meeting end as the group
had to go to the hotel for lunch. There were cries from the
audience of "No, no, don't go yet," and the group decided to
forego lunch.*

*The highlight of the Moscow visit, however, was our meeting with
Mrs. Khrushchev on Friday, October 6 at the Moscow House of
Friendship. Like all Americans, I had been much impressed with
her when she visited the USA in 1959. I felt then that she was a
good friend of the United States and was doing a great deal to
help bring about peace between our two countries. It had never
before occurred to me that it might be possible to meet her
personally some time, but when we were in Minsk on Friday,
September 22 I decided to take a chance and wrote to her. I
addressed the letter to Mrs. Nina Khrushchev, Moscow, USSR
and did not really believe it would reach her or that anything
would come of it.*

*To my surprise and delight after we got to Moscow we heard that
Mrs. Khrushchev wanted to see as, especially the women. As we
filed into the room at the House of Friendship we were surprised
by her friendliness and simplicity. No make-up, no Paris gown or
foundation, just a dark dress, her hair in simple style. She was
friendly and plain, the kind of woman you would go to for
encouragement and advice in something that was important.*

*Mrs. Khrushchev promised to tell her husband of the world's
concern because of Soviet resumption of atomic bomb testing. At
the same time she expressed concern over the necessity for such
resumption. When Bea Herrick invited a group of Russian women
to come and visit us in New York next year, Mrs. Khrushchev said
that if the State Department would issue visas they would
certainly come. She added that 20 women from Miami had*

visited her; she had enjoyed their visit and considered them her friends. Mrs. Tatiana Zuyeva, vice-president of the Soviet Women's Council, said that they would be very pleased to take up the invitation.

Before we left, Mrs. Khrushchev gave us all little guide-books illustrated with photographs of Moscow. One asked for her autograph and then all wanted it. She made an extra one for my family and I gave two little pocket chess sets for her grandchildren.

She told us, "The aim you set yourselves is a most honourable one. My husband says 'let us drop all our bombs into the ocean.' I like that statement of his best of all. But we do not mean only our bombs when we say that, but also those of other people. We have no alternative. In the last 40 years we have had unfortunate experiences."

In response to a question of Bea Herrick's about women contributing to world peace, Mrs. Khrushchev said, "Women can contribute greatly. They are mothers and they know suffering. Women at present outnumber men in the human race. If it was up to the women they would end all arms. Women should raise their hands against war."

By Regina Fischer (American team) & Cyril Pustan (British team)

Hemsworth Court, Hemsworth Street, Shoreditch, London N1, England

October 20, 1961 – 5543

Acknowledgements

I could not have written this book without access to Cyril's papers, and Ella's refusal to throw anything out in her long marriage to Max. Those papers were sent to Ella by Cyril's friend and colleague from when he lived in Jena, Christine Patzer, beginning on 16 November 2000. The boxes of material were stored in the loft and came to light shortly before Ella died in March 2021. We knew about some of his exploits, as some papers were in the living room, but not how close he was to the world events of 1961. Nor did we know the secrets the papers revealed.

Christine and Ella became "pen pals" and exchanged many letters concerning their family, love of flowers, and ailments. They also sent each other gifts of clothing, flowers, and money for medical treatment.

I decided to write the book when I realised what an interesting life Cyril had. He wrote beautifully and has been written about by others lovingly.

I have used Cyril's words wherever possible, and his and Regina Fischer's words where they wrote joint articles. I have included within the body of the book the relevant parts of his involvement in their account of the 1961 Peace Walk entitled *"The San Francisco to Moscow Walk for Peace Gets there"*, and in the Annex I have attached the entire account as a historical record.

I have drawn on Cyril's cousin Etel Shephard's research and excellent history of the Pustansky Family, *"One Golden Spoon"*, and am grateful to Tess and Clare for allowing me to use pictures of Cyril's grandparents and great-grandparents.

I am fortunate in that shortly before she died, Ella agreed to be interviewed by her granddaughter Samantha on tape where she talked about aspects of Cyril's life. She told Samantha that she could write a book. She never did. This is it.

I am grateful to Regina's grandson Nicholas Targ, Hans-Christof Kaiser, Lutz Hummel, Victor Grossman, and Annegret Fischer for their help from abroad. Ella was worried that if she took Cyril's effects out of the loft, Nicholas or his brother Alexander would come after them from California. She was wrong.

I have benefited from Jerry Lehmann's book "*We Walked to Moscow*", and Bradford Lyttle's account "*You Come with Naked Hands*". Some of the extracts of Cyril's account of the walk and some of his pictures are contained in those books as well, simply because he gave copies of his account to them, and he has been sent pictures.

I am grateful to Stefan Gerber from the Friedrich-Schiller University in Jena for help regarding Cyril's time teaching there, Sophie North and Martin Levy from the JB Priestly Library and Commonweal Collection at the University of Bradford particularly regarding the events around 1961 and the April Carter papers, Sarah Crompton from the Marx Memorial Library & Workers' School for help and guidance regarding the Communist Party, the British Library team at Boston Spa, the National Archive, the People's History Museum in Manchester regarding the Youth Festivals, Jana Waldt from the German Centre for Accessible Reading for the CDs of Cyril's reading, and all for their support, help, and encyclopaedic knowledge of the work in their custody. We are fortunate that our collective history is in their hands.

I am grateful to Jonny Graf of the Weiner Cemetery for the map and picture of the headstone.

I am grateful to my parents Valerie and Harold Saffer who gave me every opportunity in life to enquire and learn. Dad was of the same generation as Cyril being born in 1927. Even though he lived in Leeds, he experienced many of the deprivations Cyril did. He was evacuated to Lincoln during the bombing of the Northern towns. Grandma brought him and Uncle Monty home as she was worried that they were more at risk from eating non-Kosher food such as rabbit than of being a victim of German bombs. He had the same challenge of living in an Orthodox household in a changing world. He was the victim of anti-Semitism as he was not allowed to attend medical school despite having the grades as "the Jewish quota" was full. He was able to talk me through many of the world events that formed the backdrop to Cyril's life. He recently passed at 94. A kind and gentle man.

But most importantly I am grateful to Sally. We have been together for over 30 years. We both deserve a medal.